The Cowboy Hero

The Cowboy Hero

His Image in
American History & Culture

by
William W. Savage, Jr.

University of Oklahoma Press   :   Norman and London

By William W. Savage, Jr.

The Cherokee Strip Live Stock Association (Columbia, Missouri, 1973)

(Editor) *Cowboy Life: Reconstructing an American Myth* (Norman, 1975)

(Editor, with David Harry Miller) *The Character and Influence of the Indian Trade in Wisconsin,* by Frederick Jackson Turner (Norman, 1977)

(Editor) *Indian Life: Transforming an American Myth* (Norman, 1977)

(Editor, with Stephen I. Thompson) *The Frontier: Comparative Studies,* vol. 2 (Norman, 1979)

The Cowboy Hero: His Image in American History and Culture (Norman, 1979)

Library of Congress Cataloging in Publication Data

Savage, William W.
 The cowboy hero.

 Bibliography: p. 169
 Includes index.
 1. Cowboys—United States.   2. United States—
Popular culture.   I. Title.
F596.S238   973   79-4730
ISBN: 0-8061-1920-9

4   5   6   7   8   9   10   11   12   13   14   15   16   17   18   19

To
Richard H. Chowen
and to the memory of
Wilfrid H. Callcott
and
William A. Foran

Contents

Illustrations

Preface

In PREFATORY REMARKS to her *Rock Encyclopedia* (1969), critic Lillian Roxon spoke of the difficulty of trying "to get the rock world to keep still long enough . . . to take its picture." It was a superior metaphor. The cowboy hero will not keep still either, but here it is not especially important that he should pose long or smile prettily. I am concerned with his image and the uses to which it has been put by various people in various media. There can be no definitive treatment of this sort of thing, as any student of popular culture knows, and I do not aspire to one. What I have attempted is an excursion into the American mind, selecting for transportation a reliable vehicle with considerable mileage on it. In doing so, I have accepted the proposition that by examining our heroes we learn about ourselves. To that extent this book is less about cowboys than it is about you and me.

These chapters reflect a topical approach to the problem of cowboy imagery. They assume that the reader is conversant with the principal artifacts of cowboy Americana, and so they are more interpretive than descriptive. The excursion is brief because it bypasses — or tries to bypass — most of the familiar

PREFACE

trails. A chronology is appended for the convenience of the reader accustomed to more conventional approaches.

Authorial devoirs require thanks to Norman L. Crockett and David Harry Miller, my colleagues in the Department of History, University of Oklahoma, for their continued encouragement and for their support of popular culture as an item in the curriculum of our discipline; to Richard W. Etulain, of the Department of History, University of New Mexico, for his steadfast belief in the worth of studying imagery; to Gene M. Gressley, director of the School of American Studies, University of Wyoming, for his insights into the problems of cowboy historiography; to Stephen I. Thompson, of the Department of Anthropology, University of Oklahoma, for his many kindnesses, both personal and professional; to Steve Mathis, of Alhambra, California, and Bart Bush, of Norman, Oklahoma, for their assistance in securing research materials; to graduate students Wayne H. Gossard, Jr., and Michael C. Morton for taking the time, amidst their own explorations of cowboy imagery, to listen; and to Mary Roland and Martha Penisten for typing the manuscript.

WILLIAM W. SAVAGE, JR.

Norman, Oklahoma

The Cowboy Hero

Don't you want to be a cowboy
and wear fuzzy pants?
　　　　　　　　 — Line from Our Gang,
　　　　 Choo-Choo (Roach-MGM, 1932)

·1·
History, Culture, and the Cowboy Image

THE COWBOY CERTAINLY does not appear to have been lost in American history or culture. Indeed, he has been the object of simultaneous reverence and almost microscopic scrutiny, and scholars and buffs alike have examined and displayed virtually every aspect of his existence, from the clothes he wore to the horses he rode, the job he did, and the quality of the life he led. As a representative of an occupational group he has received perhaps more attention than any other worker in the history of the world, and it is a rare American history text that does not acknowledge his presence on the western landscape. Yet, despite the tomes that commemorate him, the cowboy remains the invisible man in our national past, for, while we know almost exactly what he did, we have no very clear historical idea of who he was.[1]

The cowboy in various guises is popularly accepted by Americans as a symbol, indicative of his stature as myth. He

[1] Philip Ashton Rollins, *The Cowboy,* rev. ed. (New York: Charles Scribner's Sons, 1936), is a standard item, often reprinted, that illustrates how much — and how little — is known about cowboys.

represents rugged individualism in beer commercials, unadorned masculinity in cigarette advertising, and ultimate heroism in fiction and film. He needs no proper identification because his clothes give him away, and so does his demeanor; he is immediately recognizable, and in popular entertainments there is seldom doubt about what his responses will be in given situations. Because his image is so firmly fixed in the popular mind, scholars must mention him, even if their references to the fact of his existence are cursory and add little to our knowledge of him. His appearance in texts is mandatory because readers steeped in his myth expect to find him there.

The romanticized view of the cowboy is less prevalent than it once was, since truth is the historian's stock in trade and myths are his principal enemies. But the historian's influence seldom extends into society beyond the texts he writes for the hasty perusal of freshmen, and the public will preserve its myths elsewhere. Thus the historian's statements that cowboy life was "dirty and hard" or that cowboys came in colors other than white may be revelations to the undergraduate, but they cannot negate the lessons learned from a lifetime of exposure to comic-book, radio, motion-picture, and television cowboys.[2]

Specifically the historiography of the cowboy does not abound with valid points. The sophisticated methodologies that historians are wont to apply to the examination of other historical problems have not been applied to the study of the

[2] Norman A. Graebner, Gilbert C. Fite, and Philip L. White, *A History of the American People*, 2d ed. (New York: McGraw-Hill Book Company, 1975), 2:485. On the other hand, the romantic view obtains in John A. Garraty, *The American Nation: A History of the United States Since 1865*, 2d ed. (New York: Harper & Row, 1971), pp. 79-80. Falling somewhere between these two textbooks is Samuel Eliot Morison, Henry Steele Commager, and William E. Leuchtenburg, *A Concise History of the American Republic* (New York: Oxford University Press, 1977), p. 402, a text designed for popular consumption. The best recent example of textual myth breaking is Patrick Gerster and Nicholas Cords, *Myth in American History* (Encino, Calif.: Glencoe Press, 1977), pp. 170-75.

cowboy, for several reasons. There is, of course, some difficulty with sources, inasmuch as the cowboy did not often create the sorts of documents that historians find useful, if indeed he created any documents at all. There are representative cowboys like Charlie Siringo, Andy Adams, and "Teddy Blue" Abbott — representative because they published memoirs of the kind that are widely reprinted and easily available to writers wishing to generalize about cowboy history — and they are mentioned frequently as models for all cowboys.[3] Just as the Roman historians of each generation reexamine, even to the point of retranslating, the works of Tacitus or Caesar to draw fresh conclusions about Roman life, so, too, do western historians sift again and again the venerable texts of Adams and Siringo in search of something new. Roman historians, however, have available the collaboration and corroboration of other disciplines, notably archaeology, numismatics, epigraphy, and paleography; they have reference to a larger historical context and labor in a demanding environment and must be cautious. Western historians do not know those restraints, perhaps because, in the cowboy, they are dealing at bottom with an image.[4]

[3] Charles A. Siringo, A Texas Cow Boy; or, Fifteen Years on the Hurricane Deck of a Spanish Pony (Chicago: Rand, McNally & Co., 1886); Andy Adams, The Log of a Cowboy (Boston: Houghton Mifflin Company, 1903); and E. C. Abbott ("Teddy Blue") and Helena Huntington Smith, We Pointed Them North: Recollections of a Cowpuncher, new ed. (Norman: University of Oklahoma Press, 1955). For an example of the use of representative cowboys see Howard R. Lamar, The Trader on the American Frontier: Myth's Victim (College Station: Texas A&M University Press, 1977), pp. 41-48.

[4] The interrelationship of the cowboy myth and cowboy history is explained nicely in Robert V. Hine, The American West: An Interpretive History (Boston: Little, Brown and Company, 1973), chap. 9. A mandatory caution is Don D. Walker, "Riders and Reality: A Philosophical Problem in the Historiography of the Cattle Trade," Western Historical Quarterly 9 (April, 1978): 163-79.

Much of what emerges as cowboy scholarship is itself imagerial; that is, it is conjecture offered as fact, speculation passed off as history and allowed to stand as though the burden of proof lay in other, more significant cultural quarters. The fiction of the 5,000 black cowboys is a case in point, and it bears reviewing.

To be sure, there were black cowboys participating in the western range-cattle industry between 1865 and 1900. There were Mexican and Indian cowboys as well. We know this because photographs occasionally reveal their presence. But there is no such thing as cowboy demography, and no one knows how many cowboys there were, or how they were distributed by age, ethnic origin, or geographical location. The life of the cowboy hardly lent itself to careful observation by outsiders, to say nothing of statistical analysis by anybody, and cattlemen in search of profits in an opportunity-oriented business environment seldom kept personal records about their employees, most of whom were hired on a seasonal basis.[5] These considerations notwithstanding, Philip Durham and Everett L. Jones, members of the English faculty of the University of California at Los Angeles, published a book in 1965 about black cowboys in which they revealed that perhaps more than 5,000 blacks were employed among the 35,000 cowboys who followed the cattle trails north from Texas after the Civil War. Theirs was an assumption, clearly labeled as such, but since their book was based on it, the assumption was widely accepted as a conclusion.[6]

[5] Cattlemen were interested in making money — and saving it. That meant getting by with as few cowboys as possible and paying them as little as possible. Gene M. Gressley, *Bankers and Cattlemen* (New York: Alfred A. Knopf, 1966), pp. 150-51. See also Jimmy M. Skaggs, *The Cattle-trailing Industry: Between Supply and Demand, 1866-1890* (Lawrence: University Press of Kansas, 1973), pp. 10-11.

[6] Philip Durham and Everett L. Jones, *The Negro Cowboys* (New York: Dodd, Mead & Company, 1965), pp. 44-45.

What was their basis for making even an assumption? Durham and Jones cited as their principal statistical authority an autobiographical essay by George W. Saunders published in 1925 in a collection of cowboy reminiscences edited by J. Marvin Hunter, a standard collection well known to western historians.[7] Saunders was president of the Old Time Trail Drivers' Association, an organization that he founded to preserve the lore of the range and to perpetuate the myth of the cowboy, and he was one of Philip Ashton Rollins's principal informants. Saunders was concerned that the membership of the association was not as large as it should be, and to prove his point he manufactured some numbers. "From 1868 to 1895," said he, "it is estimated that fully 35,000 men went up the trail with herds, if the number of men computed by the number of cattle driven is correct."[8]

Here we have illustrated a major methodological problem in cowboy studies: nobody counted cowboys, but people did try to count cows. Cattle meant money, and whenever money is to be made, quantification, or at least the suggestion of it, becomes essential. Men might have been necessary for the conduct of the cattle trade, but they were ultimately less important than the animals they tended; men could be hired anywhere and at any time (at least in theory) for only a few dollars a month, and it was hardly crucial for anyone to keep track of them.[9]

In any case, Saunders fell victim to what David Hackett Fischer has described as the fallacy of the prevalent proof when he referred to the existence of 35,000 cowboys. Who estimated that there were 35,000? Saunders did not say. If

[7] George W. Saunders, "Reflections of the Trail," in *The Trail Drivers of Texas*, comp. and ed. J. Marvin Hunter (Nashville, Tenn.: Cokesbury Press, 1925), pp. 426-54.

[8] Ibid., p. 453.

[9] See Gressley, *Bankers and Cattlemen*, pp. 121 ff.

the number of cowboys was indeed calculated by the number of animals they drove, then how many cattle went up the trail, and how many cowboys generally worked a herd? Again, Saunders did not say.[10] Modern estimates of total cattle, when they are made at all, waver between four and six million head, but that creates further problems.[11] Saunders guessed that one-third of the 35,000 cowboys had made more than one trip up the trail. Modern sources set the average size of trail herds at 2,000 to 2,500 head, each tended by a trail crew of eight or ten cowboys. If each cowboy made only one trip, then the following figures result:

Total Cattle	Herd Base	Number of Herds	Trail Crew	Total Cowboys
4,000,000	2,000-2,500	2,000-1,600	8	16,000-12,800
4,000,000	2,000-2,500	2,000-1,600	10	20,000-16,000
6,000,000	2,000-2,500	3,000-2,400	8	24,000-19,200
6,000,000	2,000-2,500	3,000-2,400	10	30,000-24,000

But if one-third of the cowboys made more than one trip, then the figures in the last column would be even smaller, and all of them already fall considerably below Saunders's 35,000. And if one tries it the other way around, accepting Saunders's

[10] In the first chapter of the revised edition of *The Cowboy*, Philip Ashton Rollins presented annual estimates of the number of northbound cattle, 1866-85, that pushed the total to nearly six million. He stated in an appendix that the figures had come from Saunders, who had consulted with Charles Goodnight on the matter.

[11] Edward Everett Dale, in *The Range Cattle Industry: Ranching on the Great Plains from 1865 to 1925*, new ed. (Norman: University of Oklahoma Press, 1960), p. 42, observed that "no one can say with any degree of accuracy" how many cattle went up the trail. See also Ernest Staples Osgood, *The Day of the Cattleman* (Minneapolis: University of Minnesota Press, 1929), chap. 2; and Louis Pelzer, *The Cattlemen's Frontier* (Glendale, Calif.: The Arthur H. Clark Company, 1926), pp. 37-50.

estimate and the various modern estimates of herd size and trail-crew size, then the total number of northbound cattle soars by more than 59 percent, resulting in a figure that cannot be sustained by either nineteenth- or twentieth-century sources. It is interesting to note, however, that Joe B. Frantz and Julian Ernest Choate, Jr., writing a decade earlier than Durham and Jones, stated flatly, without citing any evidence whatsoever, that there had been 40,000 cowboys on the trail.[12]

Having incorporated Saunders's estimate, Durham and Jones made sweeping concessions to the number of Mexican cowboys who rode the trail and presented their 5,000 black cowboys as a conservative figure, remarking in the process that the average trail crew of 8 cowboys contained 2 or 3 blacks. Again the arithmetic simply does not work. If the ethnic composition of trail crews is supposed to correspond to the ethnic composition of the total cowboy population (and Durham and Jones suggest that it is), then blacks comprised 25 to 37.5 percent of the total work force, which means that between 8,750 and 13,125 of Saunders's 35,000 cowboys were black. If one discounts all these statistics as unworkable, which they certainly are, then Durham and Jones are left with representative cowboys of their own — Isom Dart, Nat Love, Bill Pickett, and a handful of other blacks about whom something of substance is known.[13] In the entire book only 83 of the presumed 5,000 black cowboys are mentioned by name.

The impact of the Durham and Jones book would be diffi-

[12] Joe B. Frantz and Julian Ernest Choate, Jr., *The American Cowboy: The Myth and the Reality* (Norman: University of Oklahoma Press, 1955), p. 34.

[13] But not much. See, for example, Nat Love, *The Life and Adventures of Nat Love*, new ed. (New York: Arno Press, 1968); and Bailey C. Hanes, *Bill Pickett, Bulldogger: The Biography of a Black Cowboy* (Norman: University of Oklahoma Press, 1977).

cult to overestimate. Reviewers were quick to speak of its importance, and the dean of western American historians endorsed it and incorporated its "findings" into a revised edition of his standard textbook. The authors prepared a juvenile version which was published in 1966, demonstrating its utility in elementary- and secondary-school history courses.[14] But one imagines that the acceptance of the work had more to do with its timeliness for emerging popular interest in ethnic studies than with its potential as a model for scholarship. On the one hand it is surely a splendid example of the pragmatic fallacy in historical writing, in that it "selects useful facts — immediately and directly useful facts — in the service of a social cause," but on the other hand it is a prime example of the deficiencies of cowboy scholarship.[15]

The quality of cowboy research is not commensurate with its quantity; indeed, the disparity between the two is perhaps greater in this aspect of western history than in any other. It might be argued that the cowboy would not be worth the effort of serious study or that the disadvantages of research could outweigh the benefits that would derive to society through the

[14] Philip Durham and Everett L. Jones, *The Adventures of the Negro Cowboys* (New York: Dodd, Mead & Company, 1966). See Ray Allen Billington, *Westward Expansion: A History of the American Frontier,* 4th ed. (New York: Macmillan Publishing Co., 1974), pp. 593, 789; Kent L. Steckmesser, *The Westward Movement: A Short History* (New York: McGraw-Hill Book Company, 1969), p. 393; and William Loren Katz, *The Black West,* rev. ed. (Garden City, N.Y.: Anchor Books, 1973), chap. 6.

[15] David Hackett Fischer, *Historians' Fallacies: Toward a Logic of Historical Thought* (New York: Harper & Row, 1970), p. 82. Kenneth W. Porter, in "Negro Labor in the Western Cattle Industry, 1866-1900," *Labor History* 10 (Summer, 1969): 347-48, also accepts Saunders' estimates but seems more aware of the limitations of the sources. Working from spotty evidence, he is willing to estimate that 25 percent of all cowboys were black. He acknowledges that few ranchers or trail drivers kept lists of employees.

careful delineation of the cowboy as a facet of American culture. It may be true that many more important frontier occupations await adequate historical treatment, but eventually cowboy history must be written because the cowboy's life covered a phase in the economic development of the West, and while ignoring it might not be tantamount to omitting the eastern worker from discussions of nineteenth-century industrialization, the neglect would be serious.

The standard works on the subject reveal very little about the sorts of people who became cowboys. Frantz and Choate tell us, for example, that cowboys were generally young and that they could ride horses and handle cattle.[16] A cursory examination of the biographies in Hunter's collection suggests that the first statement is accurate, and as for the second, one might well imagine that cowboys would have the requisite skills to perform their jobs. There is a good deal more that might be known about them, simply through careful analysis of the published sources. Cowboy history is as much an economic problem as a cultural one and should be treated as such, with the same sophisticated methodologies as those that are applied to other economic problems.

A study of the cowboy as an economic factor might take any of several directions. It would be interesting to know something of the motivation of people who became cowboys. Contemporary observers of the cowboy were usually silent on this issue, but contemporary observers rarely demonstrated a grasp of general economic conditions. What occupational alternatives were available to young men in Texas or elsewhere in the West after the Civil War? Many homegrown cowboys appear to have been the sons of small farmers. Did the attraction of cowboy life — not to Europeans but to Americans — lie in the fact that it offered merely a change of scenery or, as some

16 Frantz and Choate, *The American Cowboy,* p. 36.

suggest, a chance for adventure?[17] If so, one trip up the trail might inded have been sufficient, serving the same purpose for youngsters from a depressed rural environment that the grand tour served for the children of wealthy families elsewhere. But how many cowboys made only one trip, and what did they do afterward? If Saunders was accurate in his assertion that two of every three cowboys went on trail drives only once, then there would appear to be some basis for evaluating the pattern of employment in the West generally. Perhaps, however, cowboy life offered something of an escape from a future on the family farm. Analysis of motivation might reveal a great deal about the attractions of cowboy life as an avenue to gainful employment in economic ventures in other parts of the country. Studies of immigration — and the cowboy, on the trail at least, was both an immigrant and an emigrant — emphasize factors that repel people from one area as well as those that attract them to another, and one might ask to some advantage whether or not the prospective cowboy was subject to comparable amounts of "push and pull" or whether one factor or set of factors outweighed another. As for what the cowboy did when the drive was over, it would be necessary to determine whether or not he returned home, as well as what he did subsequently to earn his living.[18]

Cowboy careers were apparently studies in contrasts, and the contrasts suggest yet another flaw in cowboy scholarship.

---

[17] Europeans were more often interested in adventure. See Robert G. Athearn, *Westward the Briton* (New York: Charles Scribner's Sons, 1953).

18. See Ray Allen Billington, *America's Frontier Heritage* (New York: Holt, Rinehart and Winston, 1966), chapter 9; and George W. Pierson, *The Moving American* (New York: Alfred A. Knopf, 1973). What geographers call "residence histories" may provide clues. See John C. Hudson, "Theory and Methodology in Comparative Frontier Studies," *The Frontier: Comparative Studies,* ed. David Harry Miller and Jerome O. Steffen (Norman: University of Oklahoma Press, 1977), pp. 11-31.

Generalizations about the cowboy as an economic entity often result in the creation of a conceptual monolith, as in the case of Lewis Atherton's study of cattlemen, which draws sharp distinctions between those entrepreneurs and their employees.[19] Yet at second glance the distinction seems less clearly defined. Economically some cowboys at least appear to have been men on their way to other things, and in retrospect the cowboying phase of their lives must be seen as a rite of economic passage. There is a problem in western American history with the categorization of entrepreneurs, and perhaps it applies to the categorization of cowboys as well. If a businessman owns cattle, has an investment in a coal mine, is chairman of the board of a tile company, is a bank director, belongs to an irrigation syndicate, speculates in land, and is engaged in the mercantile business, what identifies him as a cattleman? There is no mystery to it. He is labeled by the research interest of the historian who encounters him. To the scholar chronicling the rise and fall of tile companies, he would hardly be a cattleman; and in any case he would probably not have characterized himself as anything more specific than a businessman. But if, early in his career, he had happened to be employed as a cowboy, there is a good chance that he would prefer to be remembered as a cowboy, regardless of whatever he accomplished in later life.[20]

The historical cowboy, the cowboy in the sources, labeled

[19] Lewis Atherton, *The Cattle Kings* (Bloomington: Indiana University Press, 1961).

[20] Europeans had difficulty even coexisting in the cowboys' environment, much less identifying with them. And American cattlemen who had never been cowboys did, too. William W. Savage, Jr., "Plunkett of the EK: Irish Notes on the Wyoming Cattle Industry in the 1880's," *Annals of Wyoming* 43 (Fall, 1971): 205-15; and L. S. Records, "The Recollections of a Cowboy in the Seventies and Eighties: The Personal Observations of L. S. Records," arranged and prepared by Ralph H. Records, MS in Western History Collections, University of Oklahoma Library, Norman, pp. 481 ff.

himself for the scholar, choosing to be identified in his seventh and eighth decades as one of a company of men who had done something grand. Identification with the business community, which was less glamorous, was somehow less important to one-time cowboys who made money in other lines of work. Hunter's collection is instructive on this point, and it is perhaps here that the cowboy becomes a problem more in social history than in economic or cultural history. If a man went from cowboying to banking — which was not unknown — why would he choose to participate in nostalgic organizations and otherwise recall his cowboy origins?[21] The frequency with which old men spoke of their days on the trail suggests that they enjoyed some status or prestige as a result of having been cowboys. The appeal of a national organization for elderly cowboys is understandable in the 1920s, when the exploits of the cowboy as a folk hero dominated a large portion of popular entertainment; but what were the implications of cowboy status locally? Were western communities structured to reward that sort of common experience? One wonders, for example, if the trail drive was initiation, serving the function met by tattooing in Oceania, and whether, without it or something similar, the individual was entitled to a place of respect at home. Until there is some investigation of the question, it is impossible to assume that Americans on the frontier were exempt from social considerations that anthropologists tell us affect other peoples in modern frontier situations. As we will see later, cowboy film and cowboy fiction are often concerned with the matter.

There are many more potential topics for research in cowboy history, and surely they would be pursued if only the image of the cowboy were not always intruding into things. We may

[21] See, for example, Hunter, *The Trail Drivers of Texas,* pp. 26-28, 135-37.

indeed have Zane Grey, Max Brand, and Louis L'Amour to thank for the fact that cowboy studies enjoy little or no respect in American colleges and universities — for what scholar would touch unadvisedly a subject rendered disreputable by decades of abuse by purveyors of popular culture? — but a good bit of the blame for neglect of the historical cowboy may be placed upon scholars and others interested in maintaining the cultural status quo. That is to say, there is conservatism abroad in the land on the subject of the cowboy's place in the American experience, and, according to its exponents, any suggestion that the cowboy was not a noble knight of the range may be dismissed as simple debunkery or, worse, revisionism. The limits to what can be done with cowboy studies are further constricted, then, by a persistent bias in interpretation. The implication is that the cowboy cannot be studied except in general, impressionistic terms.[22]

There is, moreover, a small but monied "cowboy establishment" that deals in the preservation of the cowboy myth, linking it with the nebulous concept of a western heritage and arguing, in effect, that the cowboy is the last sentinel on the parapet of Americanism. Any research that results in information to the contrary is immediately suspect. In 1973, Dean Krakel, managing director of the National Cowboy Hall of Fame and Western Heritage Center in Oklahoma City, published a blistering review of Time-Life Books' *The Cowboys,* questioning the qualifications of author William H. Forbis and branding the work as "demeaning to the old-time cowboy

---

[22] A warning against viewing the cowboy as a "behaviorally quantified abstraction" is contained in William H. Hutchinson, "The Cowboy and the Class Struggle (or, Never Put Marx in the Saddle)," *Arizona and the West* 14 (Winter, 1972): 321-30. Hutchinson was still mounting virtually the same attack against unnamed men of straw three years later; see W. H. Hutchinson, "The Cowboy and Karl Marx," *Pacific Historian* 20 (Summer, 1976): 111-22.

and the old-time cattleman who are a part of our Western Heritage."[23] Forbis, a journalist, had simply summarized what was currently known about cowboys, and his text was largely an elaboration of the "hard, dirty work" theme in cowboy historiography; but Krakel saw something else in the book. He observed:

The same creative minds that put together *The Cowboys* in the heights of the Time and Life Building in the heart of Manhattan's concrete jungle recently guided the destiny of Henry Luce's photojournalism magazine *Life* so skillfully that it stopped weekly publication. *Life* magazine in recent years was often so suggestive of sex freedom that I would not bring it home for my children to see. Now I shudder to think of the thousands of school libraries *The Cowboys* will undoubtedly go into.[24]

Those who "love the West," said Krakel, "are not going to tolerate *The Cowboys*."[25] Nor, one imagines, would they tolerate the conspiracy that Krakel's non sequiturs suggested was afoot.

If Forbis's credentials did not impress Krakel, neither did those of professional historians. In 1975 he was doing battle with the academics over, among other things, the historical possibility that some cowboys were homosexuals. "These scholars," Krakel said, "have no background and are demeaning the true cowboy."[26] A spokesman for the cowboy is a spokesman for America, it seems, and in the following year Krakel announced his opinion that metric conversion was a Communist plot that would deprive Americans of the aspect

---

[23] Dean Krakel, "A Critical Look at Time/Life Book, *The Cowboys*," *Persimmon Hill* 3 (1973): 56.

[24] Ibid., p. 57.

[25] Ibid.

[26] Kenneth L. Woodward, "Bite the Dust, Lone Ranger," *Newsweek*, April 7, 1975, p. 90.

of the heritage that concerned the winning of the West "by the inch, foot, yard and mile."[27]

The cowboy establishment also posits the sort of historical continuity between past and present that make nineteenth- and twentieth-century cowboys all of a piece. There is to be no discernible difference between the cowboy of 1879 and the cowboy of 1979.[28] The passage of a century has brought little change in the economic lot of the cowboy, and perhaps for that reason today's laborer chooses to identify with yesterday's — the cowboy myth is surely at work again — and thereby share a bit of fame and glory. That is a fantasy, but one that is widespread and always staunchly supported by curators of cowboy culture. Modern cowboys, by joining the establishment, are, like the other members, its principal beneficiaries. It is the same sort of arrangement that one finds at work in fraternal lodges, and it would be just as harmless if it did not contribute so vigorously — and so publicly — to the distortion of history. Scholars may indeed have a long way to go in their delineations of cowboy life, and the paths they travel will not be made easier by the impediment of nostalgia.[29]

The commercial activities of the cowboy establishment also confound the explication of the cowboy as symbol or myth by obscuring the parameters of the cowboy image. The image is

[27] Vickie Phillips, "Metric System Draws Criticism," *The Daily Oklahoman*, (Oklahoma City) December 17, 1976.

[28] So argue such books as Bart McDowell, *The American Cowboy in Life and Legend* (Washington, D.C.: National Geographic Society, 1972). The conservatism of members of the Western Writers of America, another branch of the cowboy establishment, is suggested by Jack Bickham's remarks in *Roundup* 24 (December, 1976): 9.

[29] There is enough nostalgia in the sources. As Gene Gressley has observed, "The scenario writers of the twentieth century cannot alone be held accountable for the folk image of the cowboy. After the years had passed, many a cattleman's reminiscences became filled with drivel about the former golden days." *Bankers and Cattlemen*, p. 122.

pervasive, as we shall see, but its components are isolated and segregated within American culture, so that literature, art, music, cinema, sports, advertising, political imagery, and a host of other elements exist apart and must be considered separately, if, in fact, some of them are considered at all. The image of the cowboy in advertising, for example, does not receive the attention lavished upon cowboy art, despite the fact that advertising reaches more people than art does — a critical calamity, perhaps, but a reality nevertheless. The notion that the Marlboro Man is thus possessed of greater social significance than the masterpieces of Charles M. Russell and Frederic Remington may not set well, but set it must. At any rate, only the perspective that comes through synthesis can make sense of such diverse images. Otherwise the dimensions of the cowboy as an American symbol must remain obscure. There is nothing to the student of culture that is so ephemeral in appeal as to be dismissed as worthless; not every artifact rates a museum, but most deserve recollection, and all merit analysis.

The chapters that follow are attempts at a portion of that analysis. Because they assume the unity of culture, they may not satisfy the cowboy purist who prefers his art in galleries, his books in libraries, and his advertising in the mass media, each precisely where it belongs. The mind assimilates images and creates composites, and so to understand the cowboy as symbol or myth it seems best to adopt as much of the same approach as will lend itself to paper. For the cowboy in American culture is a composite, and to approach him any other way is to comprehend him imperfectly.

·2·
Cowboy Thought in America

ACCORDING TO SOME of those who observed him in his nineteenth-century habitats, the cowboy was a reckless fellow. Recklessness could be an asset or a liability, of course, depending upon whether it appeared on the trail or in a normally peaceful town, but it was most often noticed in urban settings, to the detriment of the cowboy's historical reputation.[1] It is a characteristic frequently recalled in contemporary contexts. Indeed, the very word "cowboy" has become synonymous with recklessness, and in twentieth-century America cowboy politicians or cowboy capitalists are those who earned their labels by the employment of unorthodox procedures designed to yield great rewards, but at great risk to fame and fortune.[2] Such labels are attached by journalists and others who may have forgotten their Saturday afternoons — surely they had them — with Tom Mix and Randolph Scott and a host of two-

[1] William W. Savage, Jr., ed., *Cowboy Life: Reconstructing an American Myth* (Norman: University of Oklahoma Press, 1975), p. 35.
[2] See Kirkpatrick Sale, *Power Shift* (New York: Random House, 1975); and Adam Smith, "The Last Days of Cowboy Capitalism," *Atlantic,* September, 1972, pp. 43-55.

fisted thinkers to whom recklessness was as alien as stupidity. They, after all, rescued those whose recklessness had placed them in dire straits, and they would not have understood the label. Metaphors, like horses and women, were not mixed on the cinematic range, and common sense, not incaution, was the cowboy's chief attribute. Heroes must possess wisdom.

The cowboy's facility of mind explains much of his popularity in our culture, for Americans espouse nothing if not common sense. Whether or not they have it themselves, they agree that it is a good thing, and they will recall from their public school education a reading or two of Franklin's *Autobiography* and at least the name of Paine's pamphlet, remarking in the process that common sense — another name for pragmatism — had a lot to do with how America came into being in the first place. They would not, perhaps, make common sense a conscious measure by which to judge their cultural heroes, because it is what mathematicians and other logicians call a given: it is present in all but accidental heroes, and the cowboy hero is no accident.[3] He is popular because he, more than any other historical or mythical figure from America's past, represents the fine middle-class virtue of common sense, and in action at that.

If the cowboy functions as spokesman for the people, he is in a real sense First Citizen of the Republic, a guardian, a righter of wrongs, or, at the very least, a perceptive and philosophical observer of the human condition. The philosopher, unless he is

---

[3] In the nineteenth century, however, it was customary to distinguish between great men and heroes, because heroes had to do superhuman things. Thus, according to Ruth Miller Elson, *Guardians of Tradition: American Schoolbooks of the Nineteenth Century* (Lincoln: University of Nebraska Press, 1964), p. 186, George Washington was the hero and Benjamin Franklin was the great man, which, in view of twentieth-century perceptions of Washington's military and political abilities, may suggest that common sense was not always a criterion for heroes.

COWBOY THOUGHT IN AMERICA

also a conjurer of Merlin's ilk, is powerless to effect change, and only occasionally is there room among the popular conceptions of the cowboy for, say, a Will Rogers, an individual who defines and evaluates problems but does not resolve them. Rogers's cowboy posturings were anomalous in the whole context of cowboy imagery. He was a self-made buffoon, accepted as a cowboy only because of his common sense. Without that he would have been fit to become only a better man's sidekick. Rogers, deprecating his intellect and confessing to know not whereof he spoke, never tried to set himself apart; but his monologues, reflecting at once the frustrations and aspirations of his listeners, suggested to millions of Americans that he knew plenty — just as they did.[4] His was a timeless wisdom, and when, in 1972, James Whitmore recreated the cowboy philosopher for a television special, critic Robert Lewis Shayon reported:

It was evident to the audience... that Rogers knew many things worth knowing. His observations ... still rang true and were quickly grasped and relished.... It was both delightful and sobering to realize how little things have changed on the American scene.[5]

Still, Rogers was an anomaly, for cowboy wisdom never required the justification of a connection with current events, foreign or domestic. Moreover, Rogers could have been — and

---

[4] On the screen the cowboy philosopher rarely portrayed a cowboy. Of Rogers's silent films the best is *The Ropin' Fool* (1922), a showcase for his phenomenal roping tricks that demonstrates an anticowboy bias by portraying cowboys as lazy stumblebums who have little to occupy their time or their minds. Because Rogers could not act, the real star of many Rogers sound-era films was Stepin Fetchit, who could. The commonsense theme predominates, as it did in Rogers's stage and radio material, but it exists outside the framework of cowboy imagery. *The Wit and Wisdom of Will Rogers* (Caedmon TC 2046) contains several of the radio broadcasts.

[5] Robert Lewis Shayon, "Resurrection of a Poet Lariat," *Saturday Review*, April 1, 1972, p. 22.

often was — humorist, sage, or pundit (depending upon whose assessment one consults) without being a cowboy, and there is nothing to indicate that cowboying prepared him for political commentary, or, indeed, for anything else except throwing a rope.[6] Nevertheless, the identification of Rogers as a cowboy was a primary feature of his public image, and popular acceptance may at first have had less to do with Rogers himself than with American notions of what cowboys were, or were supposed to be. Americans had been contemplating published accounts of cowboy prowess with horses, ropes, guns, and women for half a century by the time Rogers walked onstage, and thus they could accept him, listen, and confirm their suspicions about the efficacy of cowboy wisdom. The parochial loner of popular fiction had prepared America for the cosmopolitan cowboy thinker.

But western fiction was not as important as western film in entrenching notions of cowboy wisdom. In much of the work of Owen Wister, Eugene Manlove Rhodes, Emerson Hough, and others, love held sway and determined heroic responses — and love has nothing to do with common sense.[7] Fictive cowboys

[6] The literature by and about Will Rogers is enormous. Useful introductory volumes include Donald Day, ed., *The Autobiography of Will Rogers* (Boston: Houghton Mifflin Company, 1949); Ellsworth Collings, *The Old Home Ranch: The Will Rogers Range in the Indian Territory* (Stillwater, Okla.: Redlands Press, 1964); and William R. Brown, *Imagemaker: Will Rogers and the American Dream* (Columbia: University of Missouri Press, 1970).

[7] Representative titles are Owen Wister, *The Virginian: A Horseman of the Plains* (New York: Macmillan Company, 1902); and Emerson Hough, *North of 36* (New York: D. Appleton-Century Company, 1923). See also W. H. Hutchinson's introduction to Eugene Manlove Rhodes, *Bransford in Arcadia: Or, The Little Eohippus,* new ed. (Norman: University of Oklahoma Press, 1975), pp. vii-xviii. That Rhodes was capable of better things is demonstrated by his *Stepsons of Light,* new ed. (Norman: University of Oklahoma Press, 1969). Also of interest is Roy W. Meyer, "B. M. Bower: The Poor Man's Wister," *Journal of Popular Culture* 7 (Winter, 1973): 667-79.

were often irrational in the presence of young women and, ignorant of their ways, were befuddled by them. These stout lads fumbled through countless novels in various stages of misery, managing to resolve the issues (female or otherwise) only after great personal hardship, generally consisting of rejection by men and women of wealth, position, power, and good looks. Their literary antecedents lay more in the books of Horatio Alger, Jr., than in any western tradition of rugged individualism or common sense. The few pragmatic cowboys of writers like O. Henry were what kept cowboy wisdom before the reading public while the literary dust settled around swains and sweethearts in the purple prose of a western sunset.

Movie cowboys in the B films of the 1930s and 1940s were not like that. They had the same women with whom to contend, and they were misunderstood and rejected at least as often as fictive cowboys, but — we could tell by their faces — they were not confused. They knew exactly what to do and when to do it, whether the task was to win the lady or save the day. And they could overthrow evil by any of several techniques drawn from their arsenal of cowboy skills. Deprive them of sidearms, but no matter. They would first outwit and then outpunch any enemy. It occurred to Americans, between boxes of popcorn, that brains were the cowboy's most potent weapon. Against cowboy intellect even the worst villain, the most outrageous despoiler of human rights, bank vaults, or local sovereignty, was only a hopeless dunce who could not postpone his fate and came inevitably to the bar of justice, usually a little the worse for wear.[8]

---

[8] See Arthur F. McClure and Ken D. Jones, *Western Films: Heroes, Heavies and Sagebrush of the "B" Genre* (New York: A. S. Barnes and Company, 1972); Kalton C. Lahue, *Riders of the Range: The Sagebrush Heroes of the Sound Era* (New York: A. S. Barnes and Company, 1973);

Cowboy intellect, the movies before World War II seemed to suggest, was God-given. The cowboy had no credentials, no diploma, nothing to certify education. He was a natural man, and in the popular mind he occupied much the same position as that assigned to the American Indian by philosophers four centuries before. He was schooled, skilled, and experienced in the ways of nature; he had known both wild animals and wild men; and he had survived in the wilderness, which was the source of his peculiar vision. Thus prepared, he could overcome any adversity and without benefit of university. He was the promise of America in a cowboy suit, and moviegoers secretly knew that, despite what historians and other debunkers said, his kind still rode the range somewhere.

The wisdom reflected in the cinematic cowboy character was in many instances ascribed to the cowboy star who portrayed that character. This was something more than mere identification with a Saturday-afternoon favorite, especially when the film star was particularly long-lived (in the Hollywood sense) and three generations of Americans could follow his career, beginning with television late shows and continuing through the most recent western at the local theater. Under such circumstances the cowboy star was of transcendent importance in the popular mind. Americans could conclude that the years spent in re-creating episodes of imagined national history somehow qualified the movie cowboy to assess our current condition and offer guidance — to function, ultimately, as a father figure, benevolent and all-wise. Of this phenomenon John Wayne is perhaps the best, most obvious example, and it must be said that he played his role to perfection.

Alan G. Barbour, *The Thrill of It All* (New York: Macmillan Company, 1971); and Don Miller, *Hollywood Corral* (New York: Popular Library, 1976).

Wayne, born Marion Morrison in Iowa in 1907, began making western movies in 1930.[9] He completed nearly two hundred films in a half century of work and became *the* movie cowboy, supplanting William S. Hart and Tom Mix in all but the most nostalgic memories. The common sense he brought to the screen was an elaboration on the advice his father, a pharmacist, had once given him. Said the elder Morrison, a man should keep his word, never intentionally insult anyone, and not look for trouble — but in case of trouble a man should make certain that he won. Those ideas became the basis for Wayne's film image. "Following my Dad's advice," he recalled in 1969, "if a guy hit me with a vase, I'd hit him with a chair. That's the way we played it. I changed the saintly Boy Scout of the original cowboy hero into a more normal kind of fella."[10]

After thirty years of the pragmatic approach to cinematic interpersonal relationships had established him as a fixture of American popular culture, Wayne's political character began to emerge in sharper focus. A vigorous enemy of Communism in the 1950s, he entered the 1960s espousing patriotism, supporting American involvement in Vietnam (not originally, but after American troops were there), and castigating politicians for their failure to understand their constituencies. Critical politicians, aware of his political leanings, suggested that his film *The Green Berets* (1968) was a Pentagon-inspired propaganda piece designed to present the Vietnam War in a favor-

[9] See Mark Picci, Boris Zmijewsky, and Steve Zmijewsky, *The Films of John Wayne* (Seacaucus, N.J.: Citadel Press, 1970); Alan G. Barbour, *John Wayne* (New York: Pyramid Publications, 1974); Maurice Zolotow, *Shooting Star: A Biography of John Wayne* (New York: Simon and Schuster, 1974); George Carpozi, Jr., *The John Wayne Story* (New York: Dell Publishing Co., 1974); and Allen Eyles, *John Wayne and the Movies* (New York: Grosset & Dunlap, 1977).

[10] "John Wayne as the Last Hero," *Time*, August 8, 1969, p. 54.

able light when, in fact, the American people opposed the war. Wayne replied:

This so-called intellectual group [meaning the politicians] aren't in touch with the American people, regardless of [William] Fullbright's blatting, and Eugene McCarthy and [George] McGovern, and [Robert F.] Kennedy. In spite of them the American people do not feel that way. Instead of taking a census, they ought to count the tickets that were sold to that picture.[11]

On other occasions he stated publicly that the voting age in the United States should be raised to thirty-five, cursed Eric Sevareid and Walter Cronkite, damned reporters generally because they always wanted him to "say something controversial," and supported, variously, the political ambitions of Ronald Reagan, George Wallace, and Barry Goldwater.[12] He made public-service television announcements for United States Savings Bonds, and in November, 1970, he starred in the NBC television special *Swing Out, Sweet Land,* a "musical-comedy salute to the United States of America," because he believed that "kids . . . deserve to know what their fathers and forefathers had to go through to make this nation great."[13]

Critics, knowing that art imitates life, responded to all of this by reviewing Wayne's politics rather than his films. His portrayal of Rooster Cogburn in *True Grit* (1969) was masterful, they said, because the Cogburn character was a parody of Wayne himself: boisterous, besotted, and half-blind. The film surely contained his last gun battle because, after all, he was sixty-three years old and pretty fat. And so it went. Wayne

[11] Ibid., p. 56.
[12] See Lorraine Gauguin, "Duke in Durango," *National Review,* April 27, 1973, pp. 472-73.
[13] Quoted in Odessa Farquhar, "John Wayne in Special," *Sunday Oklahoman TV News* (Oklahoma City), November 29-December 5, 1970.

won an Academy Award for his performance, but his politics still drew more attention than his acting; so critics were quick to point out that if one watched closely in *Rio Lobo* (1970) he might observe Wayne, otherwise attired as a cowboy, wearing "a Vietnamese montagnard bracelet."[14]

But the John Wayne film that elicited the severest criticism was Mark Rydell's *The Cowboys* (1972), a tale of murder and revenge involving small boys. Critics decried the film's violence with such fervor that, as Arthur Knight observed, "one would imagine that Wayne had invented it." Knight defended the film on the basis of structure, story, and societal context and wondered aloud whether his colleagues would have been so outspoken in their condemnation of it "if the star had been George C. Scott, instead of the politically controversial John Wayne."[15] It was perhaps Wayne's politics that led Pauline Kael to describe *The Cowboys* as a film that advocated, through its violence, "a simplistic right-wing ideology at a time when people may be ready to buy it."[16] This, it must be remembered, was three years after Sam Peckinpah's *The Wild Bunch* had received rave reviews precisely because of its excessive use of violence.

For movie audiences, however, the sound and fury over John Wayne and his films signified nothing. His popularity continued unabated, suggesting either that political opinions and debates over them have no effect on public expenditures of entertainment dollars or that Wayne's views were shared by millions of Americans of all ages, sexes, and conditions. There is truth in both contentions, of course, and there is also the

[14] Jay Cocks, "Well-worn Saddle," *Time,* March 15, 1971, p. 85.

[15] Arthur Knight, "Boys Will Be Boys," *Saturday Review,* March 18, 1972, p. 20.

[16] Pauline Kael, *Deeper into Movies* (Boston: Little, Brown and Company, 1973), p. 392.

Wayne mystique, which in the words of one victim, "inspires grown men to curl up in his arms and ask about the Old West."[17] By 1978, Wayne had proved his heroism by overcoming lung cancer and surviving open-heart surgery; and he was so much beloved that millions of Americans, including the president of the United States, would express deep concern for his well-being.

But beyond that, there is the enduring quality of the Wayne image and the Wayne cinematic philosophy. On film Wayne is the hard man, gentle with family and friends, who perceives evil and eradicates it. There is no accommodation, no compromise, only the sort of wisdom that allows consideration of the world in stark contrasts of black and white and enthralls audiences all the while. Common sense, as personified by John Wayne, is apparently a reliable constant for moviegoers in a temporizing cinematic world, suggesting that, from the perspective of the audience, art has no business imitating life: it should be better than life, eschewing ambiguity in favor of practicality, which, as everyone who ever sat on the front row knows, is what cowboys always did.[18]

Cowboy actors have always been a hard-nosed lot. Even unemployed or, worse, forgotten by their former employers, they know what they are about and what they accomplished through their films both for the American people and for

[17] Gene Siskel, "Duke's for Real — Bigger Than Life," *Chicago Tribune*, July 5, 1970.

[18] Non-Wayne movies and their failings are discussed in Lewis Lapham, "What Movies Try to Sell Us," *Harper's Magazine*, November, 1971, pp. 106-15, and Midge Decter, "Why I Don't Go to the Movies Anymore," *World*, August 15, 1972, pp. 68-69. A Wayne-like view of western movies is expounded by James Stewart in Bryce Patterson, "Stewart Digs Cowboy Roles," *Sunday Oklahoman* (Oklahoma City), April 23, 1972, an item published on the occasion of Stewart's induction into the Hall of Fame of Great Western Performers of the National Cowboy Hall of Fame and Western Heritage Center.

American business. In the early hours of February 3, 1976, Tom Snyder of NBC's *Tomorrow* interviewed "old western" stars Rod Cameron, Don Barry, Chill Wills, and Peggy Stewart and presented yet another perspective on the subject of cowboy thought, albeit one available only to night clerks and insomniacs. The guests were tough-minded cinematic senior citizens possessed of philosophies not unlike John Wayne's, and the effect of hearing sixty minutes of casual conversation with them could only confirm what Americans with long memories already knew: people who played cowboys really were that way.[19]

Donald ("Red") Barry was Snyder's most outspoken guest. Barry, a Houston native who had played college football in Los Angeles, entered movies with help from John Wayne. As an old polo player, he already knew about horses, and he was gullible and tough enough to have performed his own stunts for five years until broken ribs made him relinquish those chores to a double. Barry's first outburst came when Snyder turned the conversation to the subject of cinematic treatments of Indians. Barry took the opportunity to voice his objections to federal payments to Indian tribes in compensation for broken treaties. In a shouting match with Snyder and Rod Cameron, Barry disclaimed any responsibility to honor agreements made by long-dead Americans. "I didn't vote for a guy in 1776," he observed. The similarities in Barry's comments and those made by John Wayne in a 1971 *Playboy* interview are remarkable indeed.[20]

---

[19] The point is confirmed in Diana Serra Cary, *The Hollywood Posse: The Story of a Gallant Band of Horsemen Who Made Movie History* (Boston: Houghton Mifflin Company, 1975), especially chap. 9.

[20] "John Wayne: A Candid Conversation with the Straight Shooting Superstar," *Playboy*, May, 1971, pp. 75ff. Other highlights of the evening included Barry's remark that Muhammed Ali had called him "the onlyest white man I ever loved" and an argument between Barry and Rod Cameron

Four days after the Snyder program Public Broadcasting's *Bill Moyers' Journal* presented yet another view of cowboy wisdom, a sober view suggesting perhaps too clearly that in real life common sense seldom pays in hard cash. Moyers interviewed two small Colorado ranchers, Monte Sheridan and Menford Beard, neighbors who identified themselves not as cattlemen but as cowboys. However imperfect their understanding of history, they believed that history had passed them by. "About the only ones that's cowboys any more is just some old broken-down guys who can't do nothin' else, you know," said Sheridan. "There's nobody around," added Beard, "that will know the life we led."

As if cultural obsolescence were not enough, Beard and Sheridan also painted for Moyers's audience a grim picture of their hard lives and dire economic circumstances. These self-styled cowboys built fences, moved water tanks, and broke horses for Moyers's cameras and suggested that the income from doing such things was barely enough to keep body and soul together. "Hell," said Sheridan, "the cow prices now are what they was twenty years ago." An expedition in search of wild horses provided Moyers with the program's capstone and allowed him to demonstrate just how close Beard and Sheridan really were to oblivion. "Everything it means to be a cowboy," Moyers noted, "is pitted against all the wild horse represents." Explanations of what it means to be a cowboy and what wild horses represent were not forthcoming, but Moyers made it clear that cowboys and horses alike were "passing into

---

over Barry's observation that short people made better actors. Chill Wills monopolized the last portion of the program with a patriotic recitation and a few pithy comments. Said he, on the subject of Scotch whisky, "I wouldn't take it to my doctor in a pie pan riding on a bus." The wisdom of that remark is irrefutable.

history." The program ended on that poignant note, leaving the distinct impression that somewhere in the Great West the remnants of two more endangered species had struck their last tableau.

Still, Sheridan and Beard were men of wit and common sense, qualities not to be extinguished by the honest eye of the camera or the selective ear of the tape recorder. Despite the hardships they faced daily, they confirmed by their observations on the human condition what we once believed about movie cowboys: their lives were more tranquil, more philosophically rewarding than ours. "Out here," said Sheridan, describing the virtues of rural living, "you don't have to worry about being run over by a God-damn car or something. Hell, in the city, if they don't run you over on purpose they'll do it accidentally."[21] Human relationships had greater significance as well. "There's two things that you can't buy," Beard commented. "One's a friend, and the other's a wife." Mrs. Beard worked beside her husband on the ranch, and both were solicitous of the welfare of Sheridan, a friend who had no wife. All those things — the relationships, the work, the way of life — merged in Menford Beard's joyous monologue on the disposition of his corpse: when he died, he hoped to be skinned in order that his hide might be made into a woman's saddle. Then he would "always be between the two things I love the most."

Myth and reality coalesce in the lives of men like Beard and Sheridan because they like it that way, and after an hour with them it is easy enough to believe that cowboys are with us still

---

[21] Both men, however, had friends and relatives killed by falls from horseback. Their descriptions of the accidents, in juxtaposition with remarks about urban life, suggested that there was something natural, even honorable, about death in nature and something unnatural, even mean, about death by machinery.

because they are smart enough to have survived.[22] In their struggle against adversity they are very much like the cinematic cowboy. And to the casual viewer their economic circumstances are less important than the fact that they appear to control their own destinies, which is something that large numbers of Americans feel increasingly powerless to do. We find that an appealing aspect of the movie cowboy's life, too.

But there the comparison ends, for in the fantasies of the screen cowboy intellect enters another, bleaker domain. The cowboy hero enjoys no standing because he suffers, gladly or not. He is a hero because he has the capacity for violence and the wisdom to know when and against whom to exhibit that violence. It is a further point for audience identification, precisely because most people believe themselves to be possessed of the same knowledge. To that extent cowboy thought is pervasive, stimulated not by films but by conditions of life in twentieth-century America, especially in urban environments. Violence is a way of solving problems, and in movies, where dilemmas endure for only an hour or two, it works. Life is usually more complicated than that, but violent solutions have appeal, particularly if popular entertainments preach their efficacy; fortunately for the viability of society most people do not confuse the real and the imagined. But the possibility that they might is what gives violence in entertainment its status as a politically sensitive issue. The possibility is what makes reviewers skeptical of the artistic merits of western movies. And finally, the possibility impugns the cowboy's way of doing things.[23]

---

[22] For a different perspective on this survival see Bill Surface, *Round-up at the Double Diamond: The American Cowboy Today* (Boston: Houghton Mifflin Company, 1974), written for the express purpose of rescuing the modern cowboy from obscurity.

In the complexities of life in a highly industrialized society everything, even entertainment, is more important than it used to be. Ours is a climate in which ends are examined more closely than means, and critics who bemoan cowboy violence may omit discussions of its context, may not understand its history, and therefore may misapprehend its appeal. The classical cowboy hero — that is, as he existed before World War II — resorted to violence only when he was provoked or when some evil threatened a weaker person who could mount no adequate defense. He was strong and silent, seldom given even to rhetorical violence. If he had to fight, he used his fists. If someone shot at him, he shot back, but only to wound. With the exception of several hundred nameless Indians, the classical cowboy hero never killed. The postwar cowboy killed regularly, but still only after provocation.

The formula nearly always held true. Hollywood might take on any other western hero and reveal a seamier side of him, but that did not work with cowboys. Nor did such parodies as Andy Warhol's *Lonesome Cowboys* (1968) gain aesthetic or popular acceptance. Even amid the general postwar cinematic

---

[23] Concern over the effects of violent entertainment began with Fredric Wertham, *Seduction of the Innocent* (New York: Rinehart & Company, 1954), which argued that comic books caused juvenile delinquency, illiteracy, and sexual abberration. Cowboy comics loomed large; see pp. 29, 134-35, 323-25, 360, 376. Wertham had things to say about movies and television as well. See also Joseph G. Rosa, *The Gunfighter: Man or Myth?* (Norman: University of Oklahoma Press, 1969), chap. 6; W. Eugene Hollon, *Frontier Violence: Another Look* (New York: Oxford University Press, 1974), chap. 6; Jenni Calder, *There Must Be a Lone Ranger: The American West in Film and in Reality* (New York: Taplinger Publishing Company, 1974), chap. 5; John G. Cawelti, *The Six-Gun Mystique* (Bowling Green, Ohio: Bowling Green University Popular Press, 1971); Lee Kennett and James La Verne Anderson, *The Gun in America: The Origins of a National Dilemma* (Westport, Conn.: Greenwood Press, 1975), chap. 5; and, oddly enough, John Ellis, *The Social History of the Machine Gun* (New York: Pantheon Books, 1975), chap. 6.

confusion of cowboys with gunfighters, cowboy virtues could not be suppressed or obscured. The cowboys in Dick Richards's *The Culpepper Cattle Co.* (1972) are also gunfighters; they drink, they curse, they carry on with women wherever there are women to carry on with (and when there are none, they talk about carrying on), and it would not be inaccurate to describe a couple of them as psychopathic personalities. Yet when the chips are down, so to speak, they are ready to die protecting homesteaders from a ruthless cattle baron. Richards may have been out to debunk myth by making a "dirty" western (one in which the dirt is on the actors instead of in the street), but the film confirms myth by following the time-honored pattern of cowboy movies. We might not have invited the characters played by Geoffrey Lewis, Luke Askew, and Bo Hopkins to dinner in our homes, but because they died well, we might have wished to know them. For dying well is something that only the wise may do.[24]

Richards's film, like Rydell's *The Cowboys,* is about initiation. In both stories young men take to the trail to learn about life and death, and in the process they grow up. They learn what is what from wiser men who are cowboys, and though their mentors may die, they survive to pass on lessons of their own. And that is why we Americans are so remarkably loyal

---

[24] The best general surveys of the western film are William K. Everson, *A Pictorial History of the Western Film* (Seacaucus, N.J.: Citadel Press, 1969); George N. Fenin and William K. Everson, *The Western: From Silents to the Seventies,* Rev. ed. (New York: Grossman Publishers, 1973); Jon Tuska, *The Filming of the West* (Garden City, N.Y.: Doubleday & Company, 1976); Jack Nachbar, ed., *Focus on the Western* (Englewood Cliffs, N.J.: Prentice-Hall, 1974); and Philip French, *Westerns: Aspects of a Movie Genre,* rev. ed. (New York: Oxford University Press, 1977). Postwar westerns are also treated in Stanley J. Solomon, *Beyond Formula: American Film Genres* (New York: Harcourt, Brace Jovanovich, 1976); and Leo Braudy, *The World in a Frame: What We See in Films* (Garden City, N.Y.: Anchor Books, 1977).

to the cowboy. We have learned something, too, and we wish to see if there is more. As James Horwitz has observed, recalling his own youth, movie cowboys "put a man-sized boot print on your brain at a time when there were still very few tracks up there to mark the fact that anyone had passed that way. And they left, every Saturday, a pretty clear trail to follow."[25]

[25] James Horwitz, *They Went Thataway* (New York: E. P. Dutton & Co., 1976), pp. 7-8.

·3·
Horsepower

IT IS NO SIMPLE MATTER to explain the cowboy's status as hero. After all, he has no historical personification. Were we asked to name a mountain man, a soldier, an outlaw, an Indian, a lawman, or a scout, we could recall Carson, Custer, Dalton, Geronimo, Earp, or Cody. But where is the cowboy whom everyone remembers? Only the actors come to mind. Specialists know better, of course, but specialists do not much influence the public's designation of heroes. And besides, there is the problem of history, which is the cowboy's nemesis. The Custers, Codys, and Earps did something; that is, they were involved in an event or a series of events of which ample evidence survives. By comparison, the cowboy did nothing at all. True, he helped feed a hungry nation recovering from years of civil strife, and that was an accomplishment. But countless laborers laid thousands of miles of track to complete the transcontinental railroad, and nobody remembers a one of them either. Practitioners of other vocations suffered similar historical fates, certainly, for where is the doctor, the journalist, the attorney, the blacksmith, or the homesteader who speaks for others of his kind in American popular culture?

Here, except for Milburn Stone's memorable performances as Dodge City's venerable Doc Adams, even the actors provide no clues. But what was it that set the cowboy apart from this mass of nameless humanity?[1]

The literary trails of the cowboy's rise to prominence are well worn from scholarly peregrinations, and his advent as a show-business personality has received a modicum of attention. Put simply, the cowboy became a hero because he was marketed as one, in the same way that other products of the industrial revolution in late-nineteenth-century America were marketed for popular consumption. As we shall see in Chapter 7, he was introduced to audiences as a fixture among other fixtures on the western landscape, and eventually, as public acceptance increased, he was allowed to stand alone. But the point here is this: public acceptance of the cowboy increased because entrepreneurs severed his connection with history by making him into what he never was. And he never was interesting.[2]

The memoirs of the "representative" cowboys reveal the theatrical limitations of the historical cowboy as fare for popular entertainment. His conditions of employment led to almost constant repetitions of the same dramatic situations, a fact to which the seemingly endless stampedes of Andy Adams' *The Log of a Cowboy* readily attest. Beyond that the work was undeniably dirty and hard. To portray it accurately is to bore the spectator, which explains why the cowboy hero

---

[1] Kent Ladd Steckmesser, *The Western Hero in History and Legend* (Norman: University of Oklahoma Press, 1965), pp. 253-55. See also Dixon Wecter, *The Hero in America: A Chronicle of Hero-Worship* (New York: Charles Scribner's Sons, 1941), chap. 18.

[2] Savage, *Cowboy Life*, pp. 6-10; Richard Etulain, "Origins of the Western," *Journal of Popular Culture* 5 (Spring, 1972): 799-805. See also Richard W. Etulain, "The Historical Development of the Western," *Journal of Popular Culture* 7 (Winter, 1973): 717-26.

is a histrionic fabrication. When money is to be made or lost on the sale of an item of entertainment, service to history is not a factor deserving consideration. The cowboy was made interesting by merchants who placed undue emphasis upon his affection for and use of firearms. And culturally that was that.

The cowboy's heroic stature is not diminished by his failure to add a positive historical dimension to the content of popular culture. Perhaps only in America would anyone suppose that heroes should adhere faithfully to history. No other society has that expectation. Indeed, it is precisely the hero's remoteness in time that enhances his heroic image: the less known about him the better his chances of survival as a hero. The flaws and foibles of lesser men have no place in the heroic design. In America, where so much is known about everyone and even the dead have no secrets, the cowboy hero endures *because* he is in large measure divorced from history, *because* his heroism derives from altogether different sources. The hero exists to evoke a sense of the past, of a time that was better for his having moved through it. His is a tenuous connection with history, but he need have no other. The cowboy hero is thus evocative of a significant period in the American past, and that is his function. The significance of his myth — and the reason why it is so vigorously defended by the cowboy establishment — is that it suggests to Americans what they might have been and what they might yet become. The cowboy speaks directly to the American's need to get through the day, to which end history is as useless as any other pessimism.[3]

[3] Myths develop their own histories, whose functions are discussed in the introduction to Mircea Eliade, *Rites and Symbols of Initiation: The Mysteries of Birth and Rebirth,* trans. Willard R. Trask (New York: Harper Torchbooks, 1965), pp. ix-xv. A fuller exposition is Mircea Eliade, *Myth and Reality,* trans. Willard R. Trask (New York: Harper & Row, 1963). The hero's role in various societies is discussed in Joseph Campbell, *The Hero with a Thousand Faces,* 2d ed. (Princeton, N.J.: Princeton University

Such analyses are meaningless in the context of arguments to the effect that the historical cowboy was indeed the superior individual that commercially manufactured myth has made him out to be. Because the historical sources do not sustain such arguments, psychosocial explanations are brought to the fore, the principal one having to do with the natural superiority of men on horseback over men on foot. It is more than a little peculiar that few concessions are made to the superiority of Indians on the same score, but in any case the cowboy is counted a better man than most because he was seldom a pedestrian. Scholars who should remember that English longbowmen demolished equally fallacious French notions of superiority several centuries ago are often the first to point to the miraculous powers of the horse.[4] It may be true, as Ramon Adams observed, that if a man "didn't have a hoss he couldn't be a cowboy," but it is unlikely that the horse was much of an argument against equality, in view of the technology available to those wishing to unseat a rider.[5]

Certainly the horse was an imposing animal in western settings. As an occupational necessity it attracted more than casual attention from passers-by. Frederic Remington built a solid reputation in American art by drawing horses for presentation to appreciative eastern audiences. Remington wanted to be remembered for his horses more than for any other subject that he reduced to canvas. It could be suggested that his art was structured to show those horses to advantage and

Press, 1968); and Joseph L. Henderson, "Ancient Myths and Modern Man" in Carl G. Jung, M.-L. von Franz, et al., *Man and His Symbols* (New York: Dell Publishing Co., 1968), pt. 2.

[4] Hutchinson, "The Cowboy and the Class Struggle," pp. 329-30; Joe B. Frantz, "Foreword," in McDowell, *The American Cowboy in Life and Legend*, p. 5.

[5] Ramon F. Adams, *The Old-Time Cowhand* (New York: Collier Books, 1971), p. 3.

not to chronicle the deeds of the men who happened to be riding them and that he deliberately chose dramatic artistic situations expressly to exhibit his knowledge of horse anatomy. It requires no very careful examination of his work to reveal that animals came off better than men because he spent more time painting them.[6] But because cowboys had to do with horses, Remington drew them and extended their reputations as horsemen, even in a day when the horse was everyone's chief means of conveyance.[7]

As crucial as horses were to the historical cowboy's livelihood, they were and are peripheral to his image in popular culture, the linkages of popularizers like Remington notwithstanding. If Owen Wister's Virginian was a cowboy without cows, it must be said that many, many other heroes have been cowboys without horses. His manner of locomotion has not affected the cowboy's currency in American culture one bit.

The particular medium in which the cowboy hero appeared had a good deal to do with the place of his horse in the order of things. In print his steed might be adequately described and his horsemanship appropriately limned, but it all lacked dramatic impact. One must see a horse in action to be impressed. Nor is the ear an acceptable substitute for the eye when it comes to judging horseflesh, as radio amply demonstrated. A gallop or two and a snort or a snicker, and that was as far as radio went. Print and sound separated horse and rider, and cowboy heroes took to the ground to do their daring deeds. Motion pictures, at least the early ones, restored the horse to the position it had enjoyed if not in history then in the wild

[6] See, for example, his illustrations in Theodore Roosevelt, *Ranch Life and the Hunting-Trail* (New York: Century Co., 1899).

[7] See G. Edward White, *The Eastern Establishment and the Western Experience: The West of Frederic Remington, Theodore Roosevelt, and Owen Wister* (New Haven: Yale University Press, 1968).

West shows that had first presented the cowboy an an item of entertainment. And Hollywood added some touches of its own, like the "running W" and the "stationary W" or "dead-man fall," maneuvers that prescribed tripping horses in full stride to create spectacular falls — and resulted in the deaths of many horses before the intervention of the American Humane Association.[8] The horse was a prop (with apologies to Tony, Tarzan, Champion, Trigger, and others who developed into screen personalities) and not an especially durable one either, because it proved to have marked dramatic limitations for what Hollywood had in mind for the cowboy hero. And eventually it succumbed to the unlikeliest of rivals in cowboy films: the motor vehicle.

Perhaps the fifty-year struggle between horses and cars for supremacy in western movies began with the Edison Company's *A Race for Millions* (1906), which featured a chase sequence wherein an automobile pursued a train. Cars made regular appearances in westerns through the B features of the 1930s and 1940s, but before the 1960s their presence had little significance. They were simply noiser, racier, flashier props competing with horses for the audience's attention and serving to give the cowboy hero something different to reckon with.[9] But if the car was not consciously symbolic of the encroachment of technology into the pristine western wilderness, it was perhaps unconciously symbolic of something else. Its use was anachronistic, of course — people driving automobiles or chasing them on horseback wore cowboy garb and carried six-shooters — but the anachronism, like the clock

---

[8] Cary, *The Hollywood Posse*, pp. 21-23.

[9] Hoot Gibson, a movie cowboy hero, once replaced his horse with a car to achieve the dubious distinction of being the first performer ever to bulldog a steer from an automobile. See Raymond Lee, *Fit for the Chase: Cars and the Movies* (New York: A. S. Barnes and Company, 1969).

heard by Shakespeare's Caesar, was accepted unquestioningly by believing audiences. As absurd as it may seem in retrospect, we could think that the best of the nineteenth-century West endured into the twentieth and that righteous cowboys with quick draws and checkered shirts went about their business in behalf of honor and justice, tangling with villains who drove Detroit's latest model — and right in the middle of World War II. The irony is that these films suggested less the anachronistic use of machinery than the anachronistic value structure of the western drama, and this was typified by the unconscious symbolism of the automobile. Makers of cowboy films were attempting to impose upon the present a cinematic morality from an earlier day, a brand of innocence that ultimately was invalid. For the world that produced the automobile also produced the mass obliteration bombing of civilian populations, concentration camps, and modern weapons, as well as a thousand questions for which the cowboy film, as we knew it, could provide no answers.

The 1950s brought the psychological western, a cinematic attempt to talk out our historical neuroses and psychoses.[10] Palaver therapy kept the cowboy (and everyone else) afoot into the 1960s, though it was not especially popular, owing to its emphasis on talk at the expense of action. When action returned, the cowboy rode a newer animal.

There is a scene in *Electra Glide in Blue* (1973) in which two Arizona highway patrolmen, played by Robert Blake and Billy ("Green") Bush, cavort in the underbrush on their motorcycles and shout, "We're cowboys!" They have a rudimentary awareness of themselves as a part of a historical process that,

[10] Instructive is Robert Warshow, *The Immediate Experience: Movies, Comics, Theatre and Other Aspects of Popular Culture* (Garden City, N.Y.: Doubleday and Company, 1962), pp. 135-54.

though they understand it only partly, is real and meaningful to them. They *are* cowboys, and like the historical cowboy they aspire to something beyond wages. Blake, as five-foot, four-inch Big John Wintergreen, hopes to become a homicide investigator so that he can abandon his motorcycle for a car and have "four wheels under me instead of two." In the moment of his death he has no wheels under him, and as his slug-laden corpse slumps to a sitting position astride the center stripe of a remote two-lane Arizona highway, we cannot help but think that here, on this majestic landscape, a cowboy on wheels has just bitten the asphalt.

As outraged as the purist may be by the news, what we have been seeing since the 1960s is a new sub-genre of film, the automotive western, in which cowboys grapple with more than badmen. They are struggling at once to preserve the West and to survive the onslaught of the machine, perhaps through avoidance, perhaps through mastery, perhaps even through accommodation.

In *The Misfits* (1961), Clark Gable and Montgomery Clift play two broken-down cowboys who, accompanied by a local floozy, played by Marilyn Monroe, engage in the morally questionable pastime of capturing wild horses by running them down in a truck and lassoing them with ropes attached to old tires. The horses flee, dragging the tires until they are exhausted, whereupon they are made fast to the string that will be sold for dogfood. Miss Monroe, who at first agrees to participate in this decimation of wildlife by technology and its assorted spare parts, later balks and prevails upon Gable to free the animals. He does, and so ends a tale of horses and horsepower in which the cowboy appears ready to foul his own nest before finally resisting the temptation of the machine. Here the automotive device, a truck, functions in much the same way that the firearm functions in Japanese samurai films.[11] It represents modernity, and no decent cowboy would have anything to do with it.

The same points are made less happily in David Miller's *Lonely Are the Brave* (1962), a film based on Edward Abbey's novel *The Brave Cowboy*.[12] In the book cowboy Jack Burns is, as his creator, Abbey, was in 1956, a young anarchist. That philosophical fine point was underplayed in the film for the obvious reason that nobody expects cowboy heroes to be political, much less polemical, at least not on the screen. From there on, however, the film is faithful to the book, and Kirk Douglas turns in a fair if aged performance as the kid Burns. He is incarcerated on a minor charge, breaks jail, and rides away on his horse (named Whiskey), only to be pursued by a mechanized sheriff's posse supported by military hardware, including a helicopter, and innumerable two-way radios. Burns eludes deputies in jeeps, shoots down the helicopter, and climbs a mountain to reach freedom. Safe at last and crossing one more highway, he and his horse are flattened by a truckload of toilets. Here the West, personified by the brave cowboy, is destroyed by technology in various manifestations. The unacceptable way of life has become the way of the majority, and the world has no place for decent folk.

The car that replaces the horse is often a symbol of change, and to that extent the automotive western explores the effect of change upon people caught in it. Sam Peckinpah's *Junior Bonner* (1972) is such a person. Junior, played by Steve

[11] Stuart M. Kaminsky, "The Samurai Film and the Western," *Journal of Popular Film* 1 (Fall, 1972): 312-24.

[12] The book was originally published in New York by Dodd, Mead & Co. in 1956, reprinted in 1957 by Pocket Books, Inc., and revived by Ballantine Books, Inc., in a 1971 paperback edition. According to Ballantine copywriters, it is a "prophetic novel" about a man who is "out of step with the Modern Age," a tale wherein "a man and his horse defy the crushing grip of modern civilization."

McQueen, is a rodeo cowboy with several obsessions, none of which do his body much good. He was once a winner but has not been lately, and he longs to win again. He drives from rodeo to rodeo, his horse trailer straining the suspension system of his dented and dirty Cadillac convertible. He has a number of things with which to contend: bruises, failure, and assorted relatives. His parents are divorced and maintain a comfortable love-hate relationship, and his father, Ace Bonner, is an affable old alcoholic and former cowboy who yearns to migrate to Australia, where things are like they used to be in Arizona before civilization set in. Junior's brother, a land developer, suggests that Junior should stop living the cowboy life and join him in selling the West acre by acre for housing projects and shopping centers. Junior, like Jack Burns, bemoans what change hath wrought in the West, but he breaks no laws and so survives. The rodeo is all that is left of the old days, but it is enough for Junior, at least for the time being. Ace is another matter. He is too old for the rodeo, and only Junior can recognize his plight. In the end Junior uses his rodeo winnings to buy his father an airplane ticket to Australia and points his Cadillac toward the next stop on the circuit. Father and son make their separate ways toward yesterday by means of the technology of today.

This sort of cowboy on wheels is a nostalgic figure. His heroism arises from his encounter with and adjustment to new ways of life. His adjustment is not always satisfactory, but that is to be expected because he is, after all, the inhabitant of an alien environment. His century has passed, and the one in which he finds himself is strange, affording no secure niche from which to withstand the vicissitudes of change. In this the cowboy on wheels represents us all and plays upon our own fears as well as our nostalgia for bygone times. We too are on wheels, wheels that make us move faster than horses would, diminishing our control and reducing through haste our ability to contemplate the landscape that is our only inheritance. Whether the cowboy lives or dies, he shares our experience in the twentieth century, and we are encouraged by his adventure.[13]

But these are the things of the adult world. Where the cowboy's image exists for the instruction of children, another situation obtains. Technology is no enemy of the cowboy, but it is seldom a real friend either. It is simply a circumstance of life in stories where the cowboy hero is portrayed as a contemporary figure. The hero may be of greater benefit (in the sense of utility) when he is not always separated from us by the veil of time, and so Tom Mix the radio cowboy rode in motorcars and flew in airplanes to help the cause of the Allies in World War II years after Tom Mix the movie cowboy had died in an automobile crash in Arizona in 1940. And Roy Rogers's television ranch existed in our time, repeating the anachronisms of B films twenty years before in its attention to western attire, architecture, and traditions, in juxtaposition to Pat Brady's Nellybelle, a decrepit jeep that percolated through each program, providing both laughs and a jaundiced view of technology. It was the horse, in the august person of Trigger, that prevailed over the machine in these programs, even if Brady's jeep did occasionally manage to come through in a pinch. Trigger was after all a sentient being who could nibble on ropes and do dozens of other useful things for the cowboy that rode him: he could be relied upon. It is no small measure of Rogers's debt to the horse for having made him a star that he had Trigger mounted (he resents the word "stuffed") to be preserved against the ravages of time in his Apple Valley museum. Cynics like James Horwitz may believe that the horse is merely waiting for the taxidermist to prepare his

[13] In this context consider John W. Ward, "The Meaning of Lindbergh's Flight," *American Quarterly* 10 (Spring, 1958): 3–16.

rider,[14] but their disillusionment grows from their childhood perception of the relationship between cowboys and horses in movies and television programs of the 1950s, entertainments in which horses were not horses at all but intelligent creatures who shared the fame and popularity of their owners. Trigger, after all, had his own comic book in the 1950s, and so did Gene Autry's Champion. They were heroes too, and if you would not stuff a cowboy hero, you should not stuff a horse who enjoyed the same status. Our bicycles and tricycles were good enough to carry their names when we impersonated their masters, and we imagine that they deserve better treatment.

Trigger's fate, however, is more or less the fate of all cowboy heroes' horses. Trigger is only an inanimate memory from a time when horses mattered, in life and in art, but at least his name is recalled. He was one of the last casualties of television's surgery on the cowboy. If radio left the cowboy afoot and movies gave him wheels, television put him back in the saddle on an occasional basis, but aboard a nameless nag that had no personality and no repertoire. In the 1960s, the heyday of the television western, what horse on the Ponderosa or in the Big Valley had a name? Who carried Little Joe or Cheyenne or Sugarfoot hither and yon? Hoss Cartwright and Bronco Lane had monikers evocative of horseflesh, but that was just about as close as television came. Human relationships comprised the content of television westerns and were the focus of their attention, and cowboy reliance upon good horses was not a necessary ingredient. Television disassociated cowboys and horses in programming, leaving the connection to cigarette cowboys; but that meant more nostalgia, for in advertising the horse was merely picturesque, exhibiting none of the utility that had made horses fixtures of cowboy entertainment.

[14] Horwitz, *They Went Thataway,* p. 248.

Thereafter, television cowboys could maintain their identities as cowboys without ever being seen on or near a horse.[15] That broadened the possibilities with regard to who could be a cowboy, and it indicated the need for other indices of cowboy status. Without the convenience of a horse to label a man, you had to go by his clothing, and clothing could be purchased by anyone. The proliferation of cowboy imagery in recent years is due in large measure to the retirement of the horse and now the highways abound with cowboys on wheels, from the businessman in a sports car and the ironworker in his pickup to the apotheosis of the type, the American trucker.

[15] See Horace Newcomb, *TV: The Most Popular Art* (Garden City, N.Y.: Anchor Books, 1974), chap. 3.

·4·
Everyman
a Cowboy

THE STORY AGED QUICKLY after its first telling, but it had to do with the way one might distinguish between a cowboy and a truck driver. The cowboy, a wag would say, was the one wearing tennis shoes. The trucker's penchant for western wear arises more from considerations of utility than from those of fashion, and the cowboy image of the trucker is little more than a fiction of journalism; but in his attire the trucker extends the image and is thus representative of large numbers of Americans from all walks of life who affect similar styles of dress.[1] So common is the phenomenon of cowboy garb that a pair of sneakers might indeed offer the only clue to distinguishing the cowboy from the booted majority.

---

[1] The comparison of truck drivers and cowboys is manufactured in the introduction to Jane Stern, *Trucker: A Portrait of the Last American Cowboy* (New York: McGraw-Hill Book Company, 1975), pp. 1-13. The book abounds with photographs of truckers in western attire. A different perspective is presented by Robert Krueger, *Gypsy on 18 Wheels: A Trucker's Tale* (New York: Praeger Publishers, 1975). See also Leigh Charlton, "The Last Cowboy," *CB Life*, November, 1977, pp. 37-39; Max Franklin, *The Last of the Cowboys* (New York: New American Library,

Western clothing has no utility (beyond covering nakedness) for most of the Americans who wear it. They are simply in costume. Fancy shirts, jeans, and boots allow the public an opportunity to participate directly in the myth of the Old West by dressing the part, and the popularity of the cowboy image is reflected nationally in sales figures for western wear.[2] The selection, purchase, and display of clothing comprise but one of the experiences available to those wishing to escape to yesteryear, but it is an experience easily had, and it contributes to the idea that anyone can be a cowboy. The suburbanite who labors eight hours a day behind a desk in a high-rise office building and battles crabgrass on weekends may protest, in the words of Tom T. Hall's song, "But I'm a cowboy, too," and have the costume to prove it. The proper trappings for this other life may be found on the racks at most department stores, and plenty of Americans have taken the trouble to acquire them.

Fashion is a subject more complex than the casual observer might first imagine, and, though it is an aspect of popular culture, it receives the sort of attention usually reserved for weightier matters. It has its own social psychology and is, according to René König, "a general social institution" that "affects and shapes man as a whole." Fashion is "a universal,

---

1977), a novel based on director John Leone's screenplay for his film, which was retitled *The Great Smokey Roadblock* and released during the summer of 1978; and, as an example of what this sort of thing leads to in popular fiction, Larry Adcock, *CB Angel* (New York: Popular Library, 1977), an absurd tale of a former rodeo cowboy and his Indian partner — the Lone Ranger and Tonto in citizen's band parlance — who battle gangsters in Winston-Salem, North Carolina. Sam Peckinpah presented the trucker as a western hero in his film *Convoy* (1978).

2 William W. Savage, Jr., "The Cowboy Myth," in *The Cowboys: Six-Shooters, Songs, and Sex,* ed. Charles W. Harris and Buck Rainey (Norman: University of Oklahoma Press, 1976), p. 157n.

formative principle in civilization, capable of affecting and transforming not only the human body but also all its modes of expression," and König warns that "its cultural-creative force must not be underestimated."[3] If that is so, millions of Americans are not just playing cowboy.

When it comes to clothes, there are two kinds of people. There are those who wear what they like, and there are those who wear what others like, the others in this instance being arbiters of fashion. According to merchants who sell it, western attire appeals to many people because it allows them to express their individuality and to indulge in nostalgic fantasies.[4] Some dealers observe that people who buy western clothes want to live in the past, but they also acknowledge as a secondary consideration the practical appeal of the clothing: it is durable and does not wear out as quickly as other apparel. Material that is durable dictates fashion that is traditional, inasmuch as things that last longer are worn longer and are therefore seen more often. There are frequent superficial changes in styles in western wear, but the basic patterns do not change, and the past is evoked through a uniform "western cut."

Referees of fashion occasionally endorse western wear as some sort of new direction for the fashion-conscious individual. In April, 1975, the editors of *Gentlemen's Quarterly* devoted nearly the entire issue to the western look as an aspect of the leisure look, supporting their pictorial coverage with articles on western cooking, rodeo star Larry Mahan, the cowboy mystique, and dude ranches (the last item appro-

---

[3] René König, *A La Mode: On the Social Psychology of Fashion*, trans. F. Bradley (New York: Seabury Press, 1973), p. 40.
[4] I am indebted to Bob Warford, of Norman, Oklahoma, for his helpful insights into the western-wear industry.

priately entitled "Playing Cowboy"). "Some things never change," said the editors, including:

The vast landscape of the desert. The rolling foothills of Arizona. The great Western sky. And the clothes. The faded blue denim. The soft checks of cowboy shirts. The mellowness of leather boots. Here is tradition: not a fossil, but a living, growing thing — echoing old values, yet firmly rooted in the 20th century.[5]

The suggestion, of course, was that anyone might partake of the tradition for a few dollars here and a few dollars there. Anyone, in short, might be a cowboy, although the advertisers who hawked their wares fore and aft of the pictorials managed to raise questions about the authenticity of the experience. Pseudowestern garb by a Parisian designer promised one thing, but an American manufacturer promised another:

There's been a lot of talk 'bout how popular the western look is gettin' back East. But there's a heap o' difference between just a western look and real cowboy clothes like Remuda is makin'. Remuda may not have been in business back when they rode the Golden Triangle in Texas, but when it comes to authentic western wear, they make the real thing. So if you're a hankerin' to put on real cowboy duds, look for...the Remuda name. You'll look O.K. in any corral.[6]

The genuineness of the product is countenanced by the supposed cowboy-like vernacular of the advertising copywriter, a rendition as stereotypical as the clothing in question.[7]

---

[5] "The Winning West," *Gentlemen's Quarterly,* April, 1975, p. 51. For a more recent endorsement, see William K. Stevens, "The Urban Cowboy, 1978 Style," *New York Times,* June 20, 1978, sec. C. pp. 1-2.

[6] Advertisement in *Gentlemen's Quarterly,* April, 1975, p. 40.

[7] Ramon Adams wrote (or his editors rewrote) the entire text of *The Old-Time Cowhand* that way because it "seems more friendly, and it shore gives more flavor." P. vii.

But then the stereotyped image of the cowboy is what is being sold, in the form of boots, shirts, and jeans. Authenticity acquires a new and different meaning in such circumstances. It disregards historical accuracy — look at any photograph of nineteenth-century cowboys and observe their ill-fitting, shabby clothes — but instead adheres to such considerations as place of manufacture, reputation of brand, and orthodoxy of cut and fit.

Fashion is assumed to be an indicator of status, but the affectation of cowboy clothing very nearly defies analysis in that context. There are regional biases for and against western wear, and what is socially acceptable or indicative of position in one area may be unacceptable or indicative of low station in another. In the West its appearance is an espousal of those perceptions of western history that are shared with other regions, and it is therefore either useful as a demonstration of ethnocentrism or marketable to tourists. Clothing is a significant part of western imagery generally, and as that image proliferates nationally, regional distinctions become less pronounced. Southern identification with the West is especially noticeable in this respect, and more will be said about it later.

To dress in western attire may be to "put on history," to play an imagined part in some contemporary drama that owes its inception to the past.[8] Children who dress up like superheroes or lords of the jungle do much the same thing, except that the historical antecedents of the characters they impersonate are initially unimportant. As children develop, they

---

[8] See Henry Malcolm, *Generation of Narcissus* (Boston: Little, Brown and Company, 1971), chap. 8, which takes its cue from Marshall McLuhan, *Understanding Media: The Extensions of Man* (New York: McGraw-Hill Book Company, 1964), chaps. 12, 31. On the subject of western costumes see Fenin and Everson, *The Western*, chap. 10.

recognize their impersonations as fictions, for the reason that realism — as opposed to reality — becomes more important to them: to succeed, they must fly, leap tall buildings, swing through the trees with facility, and possess a decent costume. Because cowboys are neither superhuman nor arboreal, they are more easily imitated, and the cowboy paraphernalia available to children in variety stores is nothing if not realistic — to which the number of stickups pulled with cap pistols bears witness. And there is ample support for all of this in children's books that stress the fact of the cowboy's historical reality.[9] So there is a validity to the cowboy image in child's play that is absent in the fictive persons of other heroes.

It may be argued that the validity of this image extends from childhood through adolescence to adulthood. The child's cowboy hero becomes a recurrent image. In various manifestations it remains worthy of emulation until, at last, the individual can become the hero by acquiring the accouterments manufactured by Justin, Levi Strauss, Tony Lama, H. D. Lee, Pendleton, Colt, Ruger, and hundreds of others. The clothes are larger, the boots are better, and the guns no longer shoot caps, but the game is basically the same.

The desire to play cowboy is one of the principal inducements to buy guns, if one is to judge from the content of firearms advertisements. Winchester claims its products to be "an American legend," and a Winchester advertisement for the Model 94 .30-.30 rifle ("The Gun That Won the West") and the Model 9422, a .22-caliber kiddie version of the

---

[9] See, for example, Sydney E. Fletcher, *The Big Book of Cowboys* (New York: Grosset & Dunlap, 1950); Jay Clark, *Cowboys* (New York: Golden Press, 1964); and, for older children, J. Frank Dobie, *Up the Trail from Texas* (New York: Random House, 1955). Fletcher illustrated his own text for young readers, and it is of interest to note that his cowboys are all clean-shaven. Nearly all of John C. Wonsetler's illustrations for Dobie's book feature cowboys with moustaches.

heavier weapon, features a father and son, suitably attired as cowboys, examining a tin can that Junior has just perforated.[10] And Colt Firearms, not to be outdone by mere legend, counters Winchester's honorific with an extravagance of its own: "Colt — an American heritage."[11] The gun magazines that carry these advertisements abound with articles about cowboy weapons or latter-day hardware that is patterned after the real thing. They stress a "frontier tradition" in firearms design, and they cite the frontier past as justification for bearing arms.[12] Never mind the particulars of the second amendment, they seem to suggest. It is more important to have the means to protect what is yours than it is to linger long over interpretations of law, which should in any case be subordinate to individual — by which is meant natural — rights.[13] That brand of individualism is commonly attributed to the cowboy, although it, like so much else, has to do more with his image in popular entertainment than with his history.

Playing cowboy with real guns can cause serious problems, of course. Despite the fact that thousands upon thousands of guns are bought and sold each year in the United States, it must be said that most Americans, gun owners among them, know little or nothing about the weapons. The gun is a fantasy device in entertainment for the very reason that people have no experience with it and do not know first hand

[10] *Guns & Ammo,* July, 1977, p. 9.

[11] Ibid., p. 15. These slogans are of a piece with the statement of a famous cowboy hat company that "America grew up under a Stetson." See advertisement in *Gentlemen's Quarterly,* April, 1975, p. 2.

[12] See, for example, Charles Askins, "Guns of the Cowboys," *Guns & Ammo,* April, 1977, pp. 50-53, 86-87; and Skeeter Skelton, "Gun Test: Interarms' New Virginia Dragoon Revolver," *Shooting Times,* July, 1977, pp. 50-54, 87.

[13] See Robert Sherrill, *The Saturday Night Special* (New York: Charterhouse, 1973), p. 8.

its destructive capabilities. The slow-motion ballets of death in the films of Sam Peckinpah or Arthur Penn are unreal because there is no point of audience identification, because the experience of having shot someone or of having been shot by someone is not shared by most people.[14] To most Americans the gun thus remains a toy, a loud and picturesque cinematic prop, and thus it is a dangerous thing for people to play with. But every so often our cowboy heritage spawns another "fast-draw" craze, and unsupervised innings of beat-the-clock ballistics occasionally result in unpleasant varieties of self-inflicted wounds among folk who forget that the proper sequence is draw-cock-fire.[15]

There are other, less harmful (to the body, if not the mind) ways to play cowboy, including the vicarious experience of watching live professionals shoot each other in amusement parks built around western themes. Such places

---

[14] Alfred Hitchcock, on the other hand, has been scaring the hell out of audiences for years by exploiting the one fear that more people share than any other: the fear of falling from great heights. In 1976 film director John Schlesinger made moviegoers uncomfortable in *Marathon Man* by exploiting another shared fear, that of experiencing pain at the dentist's office. Sir Laurence Olivier (the villain) tortured Dustin Hoffman (the hero) by having at his mouth with a dental drill, which, according to one piece of critical understatement, "is no one's idea of a good time." See Jay Cocks, "Dead Heat," *Time,* October 18, 1976, pp. 93, 96. Because every one has had experience with kitchen knives and blades, and because the insidious nature of cuts is well known, Japanese samurai films make Americans equally uncomfortable. The ultimate use of the gun as a fantasy weapon must surely be in Alan Parker's film *Bugsy Malone* (1976), wherein children mow each other down with machine guns that shoot a substance akin to whipped cream.

[15] See the discussion in Rosa, *The Gunfighter: Man or Myth?* pp. 197-98. In the late 1950s I witnessed Dee Woolem, the creator of the modern quick-draw, in a demonstration at a sporting-goods store in Columbia, South Carolina. Using a specially manufactured CO_2 gun, he shot himself three consecutive times in a (fortunately) heavily booted foot before successfully completing a quick-draw stunt on the fourth try.

as Frontier City, north of Oklahoma City; Silver Dollar City, near Branson, Missouri; and the Old Tucson movie lot near new Tucson, Arizona, to name only three, feature hourly gunfights by stuntmen armed with black-powder weapons who litter the dusty streets with their own bodies and those of their colleagues — all in good fun, of course. The professionals at Old Tucson in the late 1960s pantomimed intricate little dramas, embellished with whopping good fistfights that took place right under the spectator's noses and concluded with plenty of gunfire and even a few ounces of synthetic blood. It is something of a tribute to the cowboy that so many of these places thrive. There are several in the South — Ghost Town, near Maggie, and Lost Mine Town, near Franklin, both in North Carolina, are examples — and they too attest to the popularity of the cowboy. Indeed, the South, having no marketable culture of its own (for how many would visit an amusement park having slavery or the Civil War as its theme?), has adopted the cowboy as a favorite image. This is reflected particularly in southern music, as we shall see in the next chapter, and so complete is the identification of the cowboy with the South that to be southern in the popular mind is also to be western. That perhaps explains why there is public acceptance of Jimmy Carter in cowboy clothes but not of Gerald Ford in similar attire: it is all right for the president of the United States to play cowboy if he has the proper credentials, and being from the South is good enough.[16] Actually the South could lay valid claim to the cowboy through the very substantial cattle industry of Florida, but it does not. The South acquires its image from the West, and to the observer who travels east along Interstate 40, past Frontier Motels and Hungry Rustler Restaurants and all

[16] "Coming on Like a Cocktail Cowboy," *Time*, November 3, 1975, p. 20.

those amusement parks and listens in North Carolina to Ashville station WNC's "Radio Ranch," it appears that the South would like to be the West and would like to apologize that it is not. But the traveler is told that he can play cowboy there, and evidently that is good for attracting the tourist dollar.[17]

The dude ranch provides yet another opportunity for those who would play cowboy. The Dude Ranchers' Association, formed in 1926, distinguishes between working ranches, where guests are managed along with cattle, and "mountain" ranches, where tourism is the only crop. Working dude ranches seem to be the more plentiful of the two. The idea is to take the guest for a week or two, put a horse under him until he gets used to it, and try to get some work out of him, for which experience he will gladly pay a fee. One Montana ranch advertises that "guests are invited to help attend the large cattle herd," and an Idaho ranch promises that one may "ride with the cowboys" and "help brand."[18] By emphasizing the possibility of association with real cowboys, these ranches follow a tradition dating from the late nineteenth century, when western ranches first entertained visitors from other parts.[19]

Proprietors of dude ranches have long understood the conventions of playing cowboy, which is to say that they have more than a nodding acquaintance with the psychology of

[17] There may be a connection between the South's acquisition of the cowboy and its own frontier tradition, especially as that relates to the general question of violence. See W. J. Cash, *The Mind of the South* (New York: Alfred A. Knopf, 1941), chap. 1. The southern antecedents of literary cowboys are discussed in David B. Davis, "Ten-Gallon Hero," *American Quarterly* 6 (Summer, 1954): 111-25.

[18] Advertisements in *The Dude Rancher Magazine*, Spring, 1972, pp. 21, 23.

[19] Lawrence R. Borne, "The Cowboy and the Dude," in *The Cowboy: Six-Shooters, Songs, and Sex,* ed. Harris and Rainey, pp. 122-23.

the dude. In the 1930s one observer said about dudes, "They want to wear overalls and a loud shirt and a pair of cowboy boots and rough it (not too roughly, of course, for to many of them wearing overalls is roughing it, and they still want baths, nicely served meals, and clean, pleasant surroundings)."[20] They want, in other words, to play cowboy under precisely the same circumstances that children play cowboy, with the rancher performing for adult guests precisely the same function a mother performs for a child who is hungry, dirty, and tired from playing in the box canyons of the backyard.

If dude ranchers recognize the psychological importance of western clothes to the erstwhile cowboy guest, they also understand its importance to their own local economies. Publications like *Gentlemen's Quarterly* say that you can take everything with you "in one medium-sized suitcase," but the Dude Ranchers' Association suggests another approach. "Vacations are more fun if you dress the part," it says, "and it is sensible and fun to shop for your western attire after you arrive in the community of your host ranch."[21] It is perhaps unnecessary to add that clothes bought on the spot have more of an air of authenticity about them than anything purchased back east could ever acquire, even after years of use.

The Dude Ranchers' Association is interested in authenticity, and it requires that its hundred or so member ranches provide guests with at least a reasonable facsimile of life on a real cattle spread. Resort or "leisure" ranches are not for playing cowboy because they have no cows, and consequently they are objects of derision among real dude ranchers. So, one imagines, are such phenomena as Loretta Lynn's Dude

20 Quoted in Earl Pomeroy, *In Search of the Golden West: The Tourist in Western America* (New York: Alfred A. Knopf, 1957), p. 170.

21 "What Is a Dude Ranch?" *Dude Rancher Magazine*, Summer, 1972, p. 35.

Ranch near Nashville, Tennessee, which offers such attractions to would-be cowboys as a playground, a petting zoo, and the "Loretta Lynn Personal Museum," in which one can discover among other things, Chet Atkins's golf hat and Roy Acuff's yo-yo.[22] The South may not be the West after all.

The West is a place for fantasies. Perhaps that is because its history has no power to temper reveries. Walter Prescott Webb observed twenty years ago:

Western history is brief and it is bizarre. It is brief because the time is so short and its material deficient.

Western history is bizarre because of the nature of what it has got.... Westerners have developed a talent for taking something small and blowing it up to giant size.[23]

The cowboy is a prime example of western exaggeration in Webb's view; but Webb could hardly have forseen the effects of the phenomenon he described, particularly the proliferation of imagery that could allow nearly everyone to become, however briefly or superficially, a cowboy. Nor could George R. Stewart know in the early 1950s how quickly his comments on "obsolescent cowboy costume [which was] only revived for the benefit of small boys or some local nostalgic celebration" or his identification of blue jeans as "working clothes...typical of the American workingman" would become dated, if, in fact, they were accurate in the first place.[24] To discuss the pastime playing cowboy is to discuss the subject of fantasy — which is more than exaggeration — and to suggest a perspective from which the West is not often viewed.

[22] Advertisement in *Music City News,* August, 1975, p. 11; Loretta Lynn, *Coal Miner's Daughter* (New York: Warner Books, 1976), p. 168.

[23] Walter Prescott Webb, "The American West: Perpetual Mirage," *Harper's Magazine,* May, 1955, p. 31.

[24] George R. Stewart, *American Ways of Life* (Garden City, N.Y.: Dolphin Books, n.d.), p. 129. The book is based on Stewart's Fulbright lectures at the University of Athens in 1952-53.

The West is a place for fantasies because it is remote in time and space. If its history is brief and bizarre, its landscape is vast and bizarre, often isolating the individual through extremes of geography and climate and forcing him to depend solely upon his own physical and psychological resources. Its remoteness is an obstacle to change, insofar as the concentrations of people necessary to foment and sustain change are on its periphery rather than in its interior, a factor as influential in the twentieth century as it was in the eighteenth or nineteenth. The West is a place to be experienced and interpreted by each person who encounters it, and because it is overwhelming, both the experience and the interpretation are deviations from the norms established elsewhere. In the face of an overwhelming experience, history is initially irrelevant simply because so many other data must be assimilated first. The problem of the West is that the assimilation is seldom ever complete, and consequently the confrontation between the individual and history is often indefinitely postponed. Fantasy is an early step in the process of assimilation, and it appears to constitute a psychological island upon which the popular mind is marooned and to which history is as a message in a bottle, cast about by the tides and currents of image and myth and unable to make much headway in any direction. If Webb is correct, that message is an inadequate instrument of salvation anyway. But such a view posits fantasy as a normal state of affairs and ignores the possibility that images and myths may have histories of their own that, in juxtaposition to "real" history, can facilitate the assimilation of otherwise troublesome data.

The cowboy, like much else that is western, stands squarely in the middle of all this. His history arises from a region remote in time and space, and thus it is distorted to the advantage of his image. Americans have fantasized about the cowboy for a hundred years because in the general context of the West as a physical and psychological experience there has not been much else worth doing with him. His "real" history, as we have seen, has not yet been written, which is a circumstance attributable to the ascendancy of his image, reluctance to tamper with his image, and refusal to accept revisions of his image. That alone makes the image worth understanding, and it goes far toward explaining why — to return to the topic at hand — people play cowboy: by dressing the part and playing the role in an extravaganza for which no script exists, Americans are preserving a bit of the past until something worthwhile can be done with it. In the image of the cowboy we anticipate substance, but for reasons purely accidental and having to do with the intimations of uninformed purveyors of popular entertainment. Whether or not substance exists remains to be determined, but the image of the cowboy is less bizarre than other images roaming the West; and the dude, the cowboy impersonator, and even the quick-draw competitor are no more strange than the advocates of Utopia, the pornographers, and the proprietors of Disneyland, whose fantasies of the West are, for all their vividness, utterly without foundation.[25] In contrast to many other western types in history or fiction, the cowboy was no crackpot, either in his own context or in ours, and neither, it must be said, are people who play the part. Their numbers alone confirm their normality.

---

[25] See Robert V. Hine, *California's Utopian Colonies* (San Marino, Calif.: Huntington Library, 1953): and, for a splendid collection of wacky pictures dealing with some western fantasies, Paul Kagan, *New World Utopias: A Photographic History of the Search for Community* (New York: Penguin Books, Inc., 1975). For an introduction to the western context of pornographic fantasies consult Carolyn See, *Blue Money* (New York: David McKay Company, 1974); and Phyllis Kronhausen and Eberhard Kronhausen, *The Sex People* (Chicago: Playboy Press, 1975), especially chaps. 10-16. Any study of Disney's fantasy industry should begin with Richard Schickel, *The Disney Version* (New York: Simon and Schuster, 1968).

George W. Saunders (seated, left) as a young man, with three cowboy companions. In later life Saunders founded the Old Time Trail Drivers' Association and served as its president. He estimated, from the perspective of the twentieth century, that 35,000 cowboys went up the cattle trails from Texas between 1868 and 1895, and thus he became the principal statistical source for most historical studies of the cowboy. *Photograph courtesy Western History Collections, University of Oklahoma, Norman.*

Postprandial photograph of cowboys near Cheyenne, Wyoming,
showing the sorts of clothing that these workers wore in the last quarter of the nineteenth century. The ill-fitting and diverse garments

have little in common with the stylized clothing today marketed as "western wear." *Photograph courtesy Western History Collections, University of Oklahoma.*

William Levi ("Buck") Taylor
(1857-1924), promoted by
William F. Cody in Buffalo Bill's
Wild West as Buck Taylor, King of
the Cowboys, and later presented
as a dime-novel hero by Prentiss
Ingraham. The entrepreneurial
activities of Cody and Ingraham
made Buck Taylor the first
cowboy hero in show business and
in popular fiction. *Photograph
courtesy Western History
Collections, University of
Oklahoma.*

William F. ("Buffalo Bill") Cody
(1846-1917), left, with erstwhile
partner Gordon W. ("Pawnee
Bill") Lillie, seated, and W. J.
McDonald, entrepreneurs dealing
in cowboy imagery. Cody's Wild
West sold flamboyant sketches of
frontier life to American and
European audiences from 1883 to
1916. *Photograph courtesy
Western History Collections,
University of Oklahoma.*

A comparative study of pistol designs evoking what manufacturers call "western heritage." Top: a single-action Colt .22 Arizona Ranger Commemorative model of classic cowboy design. Middle: a late-1940s-vintage cap pistol of unknown manufacture. Bottom: a single-action Ruger .357 Magnum New Model Blackhawk. Advertisements for modern handguns often stress continuity of design with frontier weaponry of the nineteenth century. *Photograph by Linda S. Darks. Author's collection.*

whc

Gene Autry aboard Champion. Autry, "discovered" (after a fashion) by Will Rogers in an Oklahoma railroad station, began making records in 1929 and films in 1934. He was the nation's premier singing cowboy hero until 1942. The last of his ninety-three cowboy movies appeared in 1953, but Autry continued to record until 1964. *Photograph courtesy Western History Collections, University of Oklahoma.*

Singing cowboys whose movie careers spanned four decades. Roy Rogers (left) né Leonard Slye in Cincinnati in 1912, was Hollywood's top box-office cowboy star from 1943 to 1954. Rogers's rise resulted from Gene Autry's enlistment as a transport pilot in 1942. Woodward Maurice ("Tex") Ritter (1907-74) had better credentials as a musician, and he was a westerner to boot. He was eventually enshrined in both the Country Music Hall of Fame and the National Cowboy Hall of Fame. Ritter admitted that Rogers and Autry sang more in films than he did, but he claimed to have done more killing. *Author's collection.*

Singing Texans Willie Nelson (left) and Waylon Jennings have revised and extended cowboy imagery in the 1970s through their "outlaw" (meaning non-Nashville) brand of country-and-western music. Nelson's award-winning 1975 album, *Red Headed Stranger*, told a bloody tale of triple homicide and brought Nelson to national prominence. Jennings's hit "My Heroes Have Always Been Cowboys" defined the contemporary cowboy drifter. *Author's collection.*

Yes, John Wayne had a comic book, published by Toby Press from 1949 to 1955. On the cover of the first issue, shown here, the archetypal cowboy hero looked archetypical. *Author's collection.*

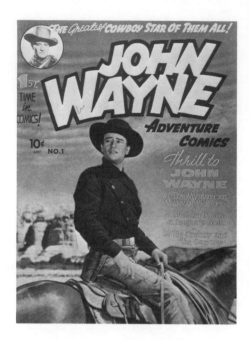

John Wayne twenty years later, in his Academy Award-winning performance as Rooster Cogburn in Henry Hathaway's *True Grit* (1969). Having delivered the now-classic line, "Fill your hand, you son of a bitch," he here prepares to demonstrate precisely what "a one-eyed fat man" can do, especially with forty years of cowboy heroics behind him. *Author's collection.*

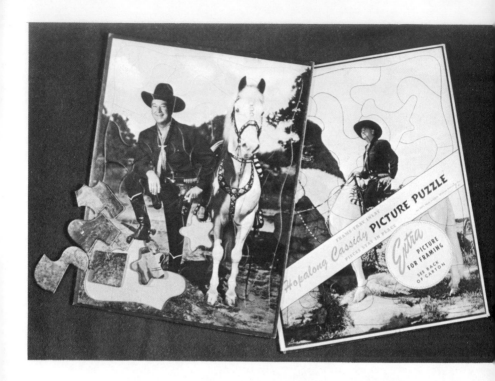

Two examples of the boom in Hopalong Cassidy paraphernalia following the appearance of William Boyd's old movies on television beginning in 1948. These puzzles, released in 1950 by the Whitman Publishing Company, bore Boyd's copyright. *Photograph by Linda S. Darks. Author's collection.*

Fore and aft views of the Marx Complete Western Ranch Set, marketed by Louis Marx & Co., the New York toy manufacturer, in the early 1950s. The outfit came with a metal bunkhouse, plastic fence and furniture, and rubber livestock. The cowboys at the old Bar-M were rubber, too, and could thus easily bounce back from the vicissitudes imposed upon them by their youthful owners. *Photographs by Linda S. Darks. Author's collection.*

75

Stills from Dick Richards's 1972 film *The Culpepper Cattle Co.*, a
production noted for its realistic settings and attention to detail. Top:
the cow camp before the trail drive begins. Gary Grimes, foreground, is the youngster who grows up by cowboying, despite asser-
tions of the worthlessness of the endeavor from cook Raymond Guth,
right foreground, and trail boss Billy ("Green") Bush, on horseback.
Bottom: cowboy gunfighters Luke Askew and Wayne Sutherlin earn
their dollar a day and found. *Author's collection.*

The cowboys of *The Culpepper Cattle Co.*, new heroes in old clothes. The principals are Luke Askew (front row, kneeling), Wayne Sutherlin (seated, center), Bo Hopkins (second row, left), and Geoffrey Lewis (second row, second from left). *Author's collection.*

Clint Eastwood in a publicity still for his production of *The Outlaw
Josey Wales* (1976). Seven years as a cowboy on CBS Television's
"Rawhide" made Eastwood's face familiar to audiences, but Sergio
Leone's spaghetti westerns made him an international star. *The
Outlaw Josey Wales* marked an infrequent return to the sort of
cowboy role that made Eastwood famous. *Author's collection.*

·5·
The Cowboy of Record

Country singer Bobby Bare has put it succinctly: "Today being a 'cowboy' is more an attitude than an occupation."[1] If the widespread affectation of cowboy dress and the patronage of dude ranches, amusement parks, and gun dealers are the physical manifestations of that attitude, contemporary popular music is the index of its psychology and a measure of its prevalence. Music presents a complex series of images of the cowboy that is a radical departure from traditional imagery; but it nevertheless supports tradition, inasmuch as the cowboy is reconfirmed as the foremost American hero, albeit for reasons initially different from those advanced by the fiction and film of an earlier day.

The historical cowboy had quite a bit to do with music. He was rarely a singer by any professional standard, but he sang — for his own amusement and that of his comrades and because it soothed the cattle at night and made them less inclined to stampede.[2] Whatever the motivation, he created a substan-

[1] Liner notes, *Cowboys and Daddys* (RCA APL 1-1222).
[2] Abbott and Smith, *We Pointed Them North,* pp. 220-32.

tial body of music. In the twentieth century scholars have collected, studied, and published his songs, and their availability increased their popularity.[3] Many cowboy songs are standard fare in any repertoire of American folk music.[4] They were featured in the radio and stage performances of hillbilly musicians in the 1920s, and by the 1930s the "singing cowboy" was a mainstay of popular entertainment. Otto Gray, who began performing with his band, the Oklahoma Cowboys, in 1923, is said to have been the first "singing cowboy." Other early country musicians embraced the cowboy as a personal model because, according to Dorothy Horstman, "the cowboy image — the tailored shirt, bright colors, ten-gallon hat and

---

[3] For a survey of the scholarship see Guy Logsdon, "The Cowboy's Bawdy Music," an unfortunately titled essay in *The Cowboy*, ed. Harris and Rainey, pp. 127-38. Principal early collections, reprinted in many editions, were Nathan Howard Thorp, *Songs of the Cowboy* (Estancia, N.Mex.: New Print Shop, 1908); and John A. Lomax, *Cowboy Songs and Other Frontier Ballads* (New York: Sturgis and Walton, 1910). The best recent collection is Glenn Ohrlin, *The Hell-Bound Train: A Cowboy Songbook* (Urbana: University of Illinois Press, 1973). See also John I. White, *Git Along, Little Dogies: Songs and Songmakers of the American West* (Urbana: University of Illinois Press, 1975). To the historical cowboy this collecting was often much ado about nothing. John Lomax once attended a cattlemen's convention to collect some songs, prompting one delegate to stand up and say, "There's a man named Lomax here who wants to know if anyone knows some of the old cowboy songs. Why everybody knows those damn fool songs, and only a bigger damn fool would try to collect them. I vote we adjourn to the bar." Quoted in Pete Seeger, "Why Folk Music?" in David A. De Turk and A. Poulin, Jr., *The American Folk Scene: Dimensions of the Folksong Revival* (New York: Dell Publishing Co., 1967), p. 45. Basic recordings include *Authentic Cowboys and Their Western Songs* (RCA LPV-522) and *Cowboy Songs Sung by Woody Guthrie and Cisco Houston* (Stinson SLP 32).

[4] But some repertoires are more intelligently constructed than others. Compare Sylvia Kolb and John Kolb, eds., *A Treasury of Folksongs*, rev. ed. (New York: Bantam Books, 1954); and John Anthony Scott, *The Ballad of America: The History of the United States in Song and Story* (New York: Bantam Books, 1966).

high-heeled boots — was more appealing to the country singer than the costume of the mountaineer or farmer."[5]

Horstman's suggestion that country performers preferred the strong, masculine image of the cowboy to that of the yokel or the barefooted clodhopper is confirmed by a cursory examination of the juxtaposition of those images at Nashville's Grand Ole Opry or on syndicated country-music television programs. For example, Porter Wagoner and his Wagonmasters all dress as cowboys — all, that is, except bassist Speck Rhodes, the group's comedian. He dresses as a bumpkin, a hayseed in an ill-fitting and distastefully loud store-bought suit, and he tells jokes while the cowboys attend to the serious business of making music.[6]

The wedding of country music and the cowboy image happened before motion pictures invented the singing-cowboy hero to add some interest to the talkies. The films of Gene Autry and Roy Rogers, following earlier unsuccessful cinematic-vocal efforts by Ken Maynard and — of all people — John Wayne, embalmed the concept of the singing cowboy in the public consciousness, to the chagrin of those who remembered history and therefore equated such musical-cowboy conventions as yodeling with cacophonous pastimes like gargling.[7]

---

[5] Dorothy Horstman, *Sing Your Heart Out, Country Boy* (New York: E. P. Dutton & Co., 1975), p. 289.

[6] It is not without significance that there are no cowboy types in the regular cast of the syndicated television comedy program "Hee Haw." The public apparently tolerates comic cowboys on a long-term basis only if they are somebody else's sidekick, for example Pat Brady, Pat Buttram, Smiley Burnette, and Al St. John from B movies. The flatulent cowboys of Mel Brook's *Blazing Saddles* (1974) simply have no lasting appeal, which is the case with most western parodies. See Fenin and Everson, *The Western*, pp. 253-44. Perhaps Tom K. Ryan's comic-strip cowboy "Tumbleweeds" has endured in popularity because he is more an observer than a participant in humorous situations.

[7] Douglas B. Green, "Gene Autry," in *Stars of Country Music: Uncle Dave Macon to Johnny Rodriguez*, ed. Bill C. Malone and Judith McCulloh

By the time the singing cowboy hero and his B-film vehicle expired in the 1950s, the cowboy image was firmly fixed in American popular music, and the musical genre that had once been labeled "hillbilly" had become known as "country and western." Country music had formally acquired its western flavor in the 1930s and 1940s partly because of the crooning of cinematic cowboys, but the union received most of its impetus from the performances of white string bands in the rural Southwest. Groups like the Light Crust Doughboys, Gray's Oklahoma Cowboys, and Bob Wills's Texas Playboys wore cowboy costumes and played sophisticated renditions of an admixture of traditional cowboy tunes, Negro blues music, and popular songs known variously as "southwestern swing," "Okie jazz," and, finally, "western swing," by which term it is identified today. Cowboy hats, boots, and fancy western-cut sequined suits embroidered with steer horns and cacti are the trademarks of Nashville's brand of country and western music, while in lesser musical centers like Austin the cowboy image, though just as popular, is more subdued.[8] But country and western music has no distinctive or exclusive claim to cowboy imagery, despite the length — and intensity — of the association.

The cowboy image is prominent in the various sub-genres of rock music. If that attests to the popularity of the cowboy

(Urbana, University of Illinois Press, 1975), pp. 142-56; Barbour, *The Thrill of It All,* pp. 33, 125-27; Fenin and Everson, *The Western,* pp. 173-78, 210-18; Adams, *The Old-Time Cowhand,* p. 31.

[8] Bill C. Malone, *Country Music U.S.A.: A Fifty-Year History* (Austin: University of Texas Press, 1968), chap. 5; Charles R. Townsend, "Bob Wills," *Stars of Country Music,* ed. Malone and McCulloh, pp. 157-78; Douglas B. Green, *Country Roots: The Origins of Country Music* (New York: Hawthorn Books, 1976), chap. 5; Robert Cornfield and Marshall Fallwell, Jr., *Just Country: Country People, Stories, Music* (New York: McGraw-Hill Book Company, 1976), chap. 4; and Jan Reid, *The Improbable Rise of Redneck Rock* (Austin: Heidleberg Publishers, 1974).

as a culture hero, it is also perhaps due in part to the growing economic circumstances that tend to minimize the distinctions between various forms of popular music. In the "industry," as it were, performers and record companies alike speak of the desirability of "crossover hits," songs that appeal to more than one audience and thus sell more recordings. The country artist wants a song that will reach the pop market, the rock musician wants a hit on the country charts, and so on. Even a trained ear may not distinguish between folk rock, country rock, progressive country, redneck rock, and other classifications of contemporary music that have emerged from this economic context, and certainly the performers, whatever their musical distinctions, are united by their frequent espousal of cowboy imagery. There is even a musical genre known as "southern rock" whose principal exponents, the Charlie Daniels Band and the Marshall Tucker Band, dress in cowboy garb and sing songs suggestive of western themes — music nevertheless touted by *Country Music* magazine as "the living image of Southern culture" in yet another testimonial to the cultural schizophrenia of the South on the subject of things cowboy.[9] But southern, western, or otherwise, the popular musician of any stripe who does not at least occasionally affect cowboy dress is the exception rather than the rule, as the perusal of the bins and racks in any record store will quickly indicate.

A more substantial display of cowboy imagery may be found in the lyric content of popular music. Songs are demonstrably social documents and may be understood to reflect the attitudes not only of their composers (who, in a folk tradition, may be unknown) but also of the singers who repeat them

---

[9] Michael Bane, "Hillbilly Band," *Country Music,* March, 1977, p. 51. *High Lonesome* (Epic PE 34377) is a Daniels album dedicated to Louis L'Amour and western artist James Bama. In the liner notes Daniels bemoans the passing of the Old West.

and the audiences with whom they continue to find favor. Lyric analysis is one way to identify attitudes in social history, and the process is particularly helpful in charting the evolution of an aspect of cowboy imagery.

First, there is the historical cowboy's image of himself. Folklorist Richard M. Dorson has suggested that a "whole code of cowboy behavior and values can be constructed from the songs" of the historical cowboy.[10] Dorson noted in traditional cowboy songs an interest in religion; a dislike of braggarts, weaklings, and mendacious or stingy persons; pride in cowboy hospitality; and a tendency toward blatant sexual imagery, paired with deep admiration for women who could manage to be simultaneously feminine and rugged. To this preliminary inventory one might add remorse over the death of a comrade; the idea of intellect as a requirement for cowboying; the view of cowboy life as an invitation to freedom; and statements concerning the fairness or unfairness of employers. The songs of the historical cowboy reveal a zest for life, a pronounced optimism, and the promise of sufficient spirit to surmount any obstacle. Some admitted that the life was dreary and hard but depicted the cowboy as a free soul, able to adapt to any difficulty and unburdened by worry. Others denied the fact of hardship and portrayed a fun-loving cowboy who enjoyed his work, as in this verse from "The Jolly Cowboy":

> Ho, I'm a jolly cowboy, from Texas now I hail;
> Give me my quirt and pony, I'm ready for the trail;
> I love the rolling prairies, they're free from care and strife,
> Behind a herd of longhorns I'll journey all my life.[11]

[10] Richard M. Dorson, *American Folklore and the Historian* (Chicago: University of Chicago Press, 1971), p. 68.

[11] N. Howard Thorp, *Songs of the Cowboys* (Boston: Houghton Mifflin Company, 1921), p. 87, and, for comparison, see pp. 84-86.

Heroes do not spend their days riding drag, or course, and the sentiments of the aforesaid jolly cowboy found no expression in the tunes of the singing cowboys of the entertainment world in the 1930s. These were second-generation cowboy songs, written for the commercial markets of radio and motion pictures, and they presented a different image of the cowboy. They dealt with themes of romantic love and had the cowboy hero crooning to pretty señoritas, golden-haired beauties, and even the girl next door. The sexual imagery of the first-generation songs all but disappeared. The singing cowboys of the 1930s also had family ties, and whereas the historical cowboy rarely mentioned his antecedents in song, stalwarts like Gene Autry and the Sons of the Pioneers indicated that cowpokes had parents. Autry's "That Silver-haired Daddy of Mine" is a dirge concerning the imminent demise of his father, who contemplates his own passing in the bucolic environs of a mountain cabin (mother is already waiting in heaven to resume her wifely duties). The song says that son has caused daddy considerable grief and that he would like to make up for it but that there is nothing he can do.[12] In Tim Spencer's "That Pioneer Mother of Mine," written for Roy Rogers's *Under Western Skys* (1938), son is a better boy, but he was off somewhere when mom expired, and now he has no idea where in the prairie she is buried. She is a "symbol of faith" and a "guardian angel," and son would give everything he owns if only someone could give directions to the saintly woman's grave.[13]

Second-generation cowboy music was alternately maudlin,

[12] *Gene Autry's Country Music Hall of Fame Album* (Columbia CS 1035).

[13] *The Sons of the Pioneers* (John Edwards Memorial Foundation JEMF 102).

saccharine, or hopeful. It suggested that Pollyanna was alive and well on the wild frontier and that the cowboy was her chief disciple. The songs smacked of B-film innocence and the sort of naïveté that never was western.[14] Titles told all, or at least enough. With Roy Rogers one might ride "Along the Navajo Trail" on "That Palomino Pal o' Mine" and allow the noble steed to "Rock Me to Sleep in My Saddle" amidst the "Blue Shadows on the Trail."[15] Or, with Gene Autry, one could encounter "A Gay Ranchero" "In a Little Spanish Town" "South of the Border" and listen to a "Serenade of the Bells" "Under Fiesta Stars" with a "Mexicali Rose."[16] Or, with the Sons of the Pioneers, one might take the "Timber Trail" "Way Out There" on the "Blue Prairie" (with its "Tumbling Tumbleweeds") and drink "Cool Water" before "Ridin' Home" to "The Last Round-up," where, presumably, there should be plenty of "Empty Saddles."[17] It was the sort of storybook imagery that matched perfectly the singing-cowboy spectacles of the 1930s and 1940s, evoking flights of fancy that have not yet ended. The songs were not nostalgic, for the West they called forth had never existed in the first place and thus could not have been lost; rather, they were downright fantastic. They were, therefore, fitting accompaniment for the doings of B-movie cowboys who were equally imaginary.

Third-generation cowboy songs belonged to the years between World War II and the Vietnam War. Life was harder

[14] Their popularity was demonstrated by the large number of song-books they spawned. See, for example, Smiley Burnette, *Cowboy and Western Songs* (Chicago: M. M. Cole Publishing Co., 1937); and Gene Autry, *Cowboy Songs and Mountain Ballads* (Chicago: M. M. Cole Publishing Co., 1938).

[15] *The Best of Roy Rogers* (RCA ACLI-0953 [e]).

[16] *Gene Autry Sings South of the Border/All American Cowboy* (Republic IRDA-R-6011).

[17] *Cool Water* (RCA ANLI-1092).

in many ways because history had done damage to innocence. The B-movie cowboy and his songs had helped America survive the Depression by drawing attention away from reality, but the problems of war and of a society emerging from war could not be easily ignored. A nasty note had already crept into cowboy music, reflected in Gene Autry's word of warning to immigrants, "Don't Bite the Hand That's Feeding You," an early notice to love America or leave it. Elton Britt, the "Wandering Cowboy" yodeler from Arkansas, sold a million and a half copies of "There's a Star Spangled Banner Waving Somewhere" in 1942, and patriotic gore was thereafter a part of cowboy repertoire. Thus it was possible for Cowboy Copas to update the 1943 Zeke Clements-Earl Nunn blood-splattered opus "Smoke on the Water" for the 1960s by substituting Khrushchev and Castro for Hirohito and Hitler, and Montana Slim could entertain rodeo audiences with the pathos of "A Mother's Son in Vietnam."[18]

Third-generation songs were violent in more ways than one. Beyond discussing what harm should come to our enemies, they reflected an interest in those shoot-'em-up aspects of western history publicized by the new wave of western films in the 1950s notably *The Gunfighter* (1950) and *High Noon* (1952), and by television, with its small army of quick-draw artists. We have already seen something of the popular confusion over the distinctions between cowboys and gunfighters, and music in the 1950s and 1960s never made those distinctions any clearer. Tex Ritter, the old cowboy, sang the theme from *High Noon* and made it a cowboy song.[19] Marty Robbins

[18] *The Wandering Cowboy* (ABC Paramount ABC-203); *Shake a Hand* (Starday SLP 371); *Montana Slim-Wilf Carter* (Starday SLP 389).

[19] *The Best of Tex Ritter* (Capitol DT 2595). Ritter's career is the subject of *Tex Ritter: An American Legend* (Capitol SKC-11241), in which Ritter comments on each song.

popularized cowboy killers in "El Paso" and developed a repertoire that mixed freely the most marketable elements of each occupation. "Big Iron" and "Running Gun" mingled with "The Strawberry Roan," and record producers spoke of it all as "tradition."[20]

The cowboy lost some substance in these third-generation songs. He was less thoughtful and more active, which is perhaps the best way to be, if one is bound and determined to go around killing people. The insights of the first generation and the illusions of the second all faded before the violence of the third. It was an attempt at lending verisimilitude to the image of the cowboy — since violent death is nothing if not realistic, what with all that blood — and it led naturally to the 1970s and the themes of the fourth generation. These themes were less violent but even more disturbing, inasmuch as they portrayed the utter psychological debasement of the cowboy image.

In the mid-1970s, Roy Rogers recorded "Hoppy, Gene and Me," a nostalgic song concerning the influence of western films on the character development of a couple of generations of American males.[21] Messrs. Boyd-Cassidy, Autry, and Rogers, the song said, taught us men what we needed to know about righteous living (how to shoot straight and things like that) so that we might in turn instruct our own little buckaroos. It was just the sort of sentimental statement that one might expect from a perpetual cowboy who honestly believed that western movies, aside from their moral import, are "the only way children today actually have to learn about the winning of the West."[22] So much for public schools, public libraries,

[20] *Gunfighter Ballads and Trail Songs* (Columbia CS 8158).

[21] 20th Century 2154.

[22] James Morgan, "Conversations with the Cowboy King," *TWA Ambassador,* October, 1976, p. 42.

and public television. Here is the performer who never escaped — outgrew? — his best role; but Rogers's circumstances, including his failure to grasp the difference between history and entertainment, may be our fault and our responsibility. So says the cowboy music of the fourth generation.

In 1975 the Amazing Rhythm Aces spoke to the question of heroics and their consequences in a rock song entitled "King of the Cowboys."[23] The lyrics describe childhood and the movie cowboy hero from the perspective of the young adult who, realizing that the world created the B western was a false one, nevertheless recognizes that the cowboy hero taught him how to be a man. In the process of growing up, the youngster effectively trapped the hero and held him in his mind, presumably as an ideal; now, suddenly, the adult becomes aware that the hero is an old man who, having served his purpose, must be set free from "a life he doesn't need." However much one might wish otherwise, it is at last necessary to "say goodbye to the King of the Cowboys" and attend to the problems of adulthood, leaving the aged hero to make his own way unencumbered with the burden of providing guidance for any more children.

Fourth-generation songs present conflicting images of the cowboy. On the one hand, the music merely acknowledges the status accorded the cowboy as a fixture in popular culture, and its statements are largely those dictated by the nostalgia of the performers. But, on the other hand the music redefines the cowboy in contexts purely contemporary and suggests that there are better things to be — if one has the choice. The cowboy becomes, through this music, a new social type on the American landscape. He remains a hero, but for the reason that he endures a life without spectacle, a life that is led in dives and low haunts but is otherwise unexceptional. He is his

[23] *Stacked Deck* (ABC ABCD-913).

own man through all adversity, even to the often bitter end. His trials and tribulations may be of a different sort, but his nobility is the same as it was on the silver screen, as incredible as it may seem.

In Waylon Jennings's 1976 recording of "My Heroes Have Always Been Cowboys," the adult confesses an early addiction to movie cowboys and a childhood desire to emulate them.[24] But youth slips away, and the word "cowboy" acquires a different meaning: to the adult, a cowboy is a drifter, an associate of prostitutes, a loner who will probably die unknown and unmourned. Somehow this cowboy is still worthy of emulation, however, and the adult becomes a drifter himself. He, like his new hero, dreams his dreams but can never quite catch up with them. The song is a peculiar blend of nostalgia and pessimism and is therefore typical of fourth-generation music.

More blatant is Ed Bruce's song "Mamas, Don't Let Your Babies Grow Up to Be Cowboys," also released in 1976.[25] Bruce's cowboy is an antisocial fellow, evidently incapable of expressing emotion and constantly withdrawn. We are told that he is always alone, even with someone he loves; but since he does not communicate anyway, what difference could it make? Besides, he is constantly on the move, which means that women may love him but they cannot hold him. With this as his approach to interpersonal relationships, it comes as no surprise to learn that people who do not know him do not like him or that those who do like him frequently do not understand him. Not that it matters to the cowboy, of course, because he will simply wander off somewhere, abruptly and without a word to anyone. We are encouraged to believe that he is not misguided but only "different," and we are asked to

[24] *Wanted! The Outlaws* (RCA APL1-1321).
[25] *Ed Bruce* (United Artists UA-LA613-G).

make allowances for his pride, which is so strong that it will not permit the least bit of social conformity. Money means nothing to him (he does not work, as far as we know), but faded jeans, belt buckles, and songs do. He has an affinity for pool halls, small children, puppies, ladies of easy virtue, trucks, guitars, mountains, and night life. It is suggested — and no wonder — that he might die young. Mothers are thus advised to raise their offspring to be attorneys, physicians, and other reputable things.

To say that Bruce's cowboy is merely an individual is to be nothing less than charitable; to say that he is an insensitive sociopath is to fall nearer the mark. He is egocentric, dissipated, and alienated, and he is a hero because of it, for Bruce's song is a paean to this neo-cowboy, a paean in the negative mode.

If only we knew that Bruce's cowboy had served time in prison, we could find his personification in David Allan Coe, once the self-proclaimed "Mysterious Rhinestone Cowboy," a talented singer and songwriter who would like to be thought of by paying audiences as egocentric, dissipated, and alienated — and heroic. Coe is a man of gimmicks, the principal one being his claim of having murdered a homosexual during a period of incarceration in the Ohio penitentiary in 1963. There is no evidence to support his claim (Coe once threatened to sue a journalist for saying that he had *not* committed the murder), but, as they say, it packs 'em in.[26] Coe has little to say about cowboys except that he is one, and he occasionally dresses the part. He calls himself an "outlaw," by which he means that he utters four-letter words over public-address systems, and he sees himself as a compatriot of Willie Nel-

---

[26] See Larry L. King, "David Allan Coe's Greatest Hits," *Esquire*, July, 1976, pp. 71-73, 142-44; and Michael Bane, *The Outlaws: Revolution in Country Music* (n.p.: Country Music Magazine Press, 1978), chap. 8.

son and Waylon Jennings, country-music "outlaws" (without prison records) because they choose to avoid Nashville. Whether or not they are compatriots (fans of Nelson and Jennings pale at the thought), all these outlaws look like cowboys and contribute to fourth-generation music a strange mixture of themes. They sing of lives spent on the road or in honky-tonks, where men are irresponsible and dissolute and women understand, and where one may reject society and be rejected by it.

The outlaw brand of cowboy music extends the violence of the third generation. Coe, on record, is forever threatening to punch the faces of skeptics who dislike his earring, his hair, or his music, but that is feeble nastiness compared to the crimes of Willie Nelson's "Red Headed Stranger," the central character of a 1975 album by the same name.[27] The album tells the story — each song is a chapter, in effect — of a cowboy whose woman leaves him for another man. The cowboy tracks the couple to a saloon and shoots them to death in the midst of their newfound happiness. He then rides away, taking the dead woman's horse with him — a little something to remember her by. In another town he kills a second woman for trying to board the equine souvenir. He gets off scot-free because "you can't hang a man for killin' a woman who's tryin' to steal his horse." Triple homicide has its rewards, however, and the cowboy finds yet another woman. But instead of killing her, he settles down and lives to a ripe old age, unmolested by the law or its minions. Aesthetic considerations aside, it is a ghastly story, disturbing in its social implications. The album won awards and critical acclaim and vaulted Nelson to na-

---

[27] *Red Headed Stranger* (Columbia KC 33482). Coe's rhetoric may be heard on *Longhaired Redneck* (Columbia KC 33916) and *David Allan Coe Rides Again* (Columbia KC 34310), recorded in 1976 and 1977, respectively.

tional prominence; and there are plans to make a movie based on it.

Nelson's work marks no metamorphosis of the cowboy image, since cowboy characteristics from first- and second-generation music continue to appear in other fourth-generation offerings. Tom T. Hall's "The Cowboy and the Poet" reconfirms much of what historical cowboys sang about themselves and praises their good old-fashioned common sense. Dave Hickey's "Speckled Pony" deals with pride and cussedness and cowboy nobility in the face of death. And Charlie Williams's and Shirl Milete's "He's a Cowboy" describes the hard life of the range and the cowboy's routinely good-natured acceptance of it.[28] But Nelson's songs are better known, and so his cowboy killer is more representative of the fourth generation than the peaceable types. The deftness and realism with which they are drawn, however, make them all of a piece, in contrast to their older cousins.

The changes wrought upon the cowboy in successive musical generations have not altered the basic perception of his individualism that is the common feature of most media treatments. Be he nice guy or skunk, lover or murderer (or both), pensive or open, he is, withal, his own man. Whether his actions lead to success or to failure is immaterial; the point is that they are *his* actions and arise from no dictates other than those of his own free will. Good or bad, right or wrong, he determines his own fate, and no one else — no individual, no institution — successfully intervenes.[29] Thus, whatever he is,

[28] All may be heard on Bobby Bare's *Cowboys and Daddys* (RCA APL1-1222).

[29] Even if things do not always go his way, which is the suggestion of Gene Watson's 1977 song "Cowboys Don't Get Lucky All the Time," *Gene Watson's Beautiful Country* (Capitol ST-11715). Here we have the example of a woman who refuses to be seduced by cowboy imagery.

he knows that he is better than we are, and we know it, too. He is at only his own mercy, while we of the industrial, bureaucratic, computerized twentieth century are at everybody else's. That is enough, it seems, to make him a worthy hero, even without B-film derring-do. That is enough to preserve his memory and advance his image. Indeed, his musical commemorations make it possible to say that in the hiatus of the 1970s, when detectives private and otherwise replaced the cowboy as a television staple and hasty critics rejoiced over the decline of western movies, cowboy imagery thrived in song and was thereby saved for better days.

·6·

The Man's Man and Women

For any practical purpose masculinity is a cultural rather than a biological characteristic. The labels "manly" (applied to men) and "mannish" (applied to women) are, like "feminine" and "effeminate," either laudatory or derogatory in specific cultural contexts and have nothing whatsoever to say about the reproductive capacities of persons to whom they are applied. They are words in the vocabulary of imagery, wherein these adjectives — "masculine," "brave," "undaunted," "two-fisted," "courageous" — are synonymous. So, unfortunately, are these verbs: "weaken," "emasculate," "effeminize," "unman"; and these adjectives: "womanish," "sissy," "unvirile," "tender," "soft," "namby-pamby." Thus to say that the cowboy is the embodiment of masculinity is to acknowledge simultaneously the inflationary rhetoric of imagery (as it applies to men) and the subordinating rhetoric of imagery (as it applies to women).[1]

But among the stereotypes with which American popular culture abounds, the cowboy *is* the embodiment of masculin-

[1] Any thesaurus will quickly spill the beans.

95

ity, whether in the person of John Wayne walking through a movie-set door purposely built smaller than life to make him look larger than life, or the Marlboro Man, saying nothing but demonstrating by the determined angle of his jaw precisely what sort of person smokes his brand. Even historically, the cowboy is identified with something called the "cult of the masculine," which developed from the he-man mentality of some late-nineteenth-century exponents of militarism, imperialism, and the survival of the fittest.[2] No one touted the masculinity of the cowboy more than Theodore Roosevelt, who might easily have recommended this frontier hero as a model for those who wished to walk softly and carry big sticks. "A cowboy," wrote Roosevelt,

will not submit tamely to an insult, and is ever ready to avenge his own wrongs; nor has he an overwrought fear of shedding blood. He possesses, in fact, few of the emasculated, milk-and-water moralities admired by the pseudo-philanthropists; but he does possess, to a very high degree, the stern, manly qualities that are invaluable to a nation.[3]

Roosevelt identified so throughly with these men — he had called them "rough-riders" in 1888, and a decade later they flocked to participate in his antics during the Spanish-American War — that his political opponents came to speak of him as "that damned cowboy."[4] But the vigorous life was not exclusively the cowboy's life, and Roosevelt's praise was less for the cowboy than for the masculine virtues that he appeared to Roosevelt to represent.[5] We know that the stereotype did

[2] Hine, *The American West,* pp. 136-38. See also Richard Hofstadter, *Social Darwinism in American Thought,* rev. ed. (Boston: Beacon Press, 1955).

[3] Roosevelt, *Ranch Life and the Hunting-Trail,* pp. 55-56.

[4] The phrase was Mark Hanna's. He also called Roosevelt a "wild man."

not begin with Roosevelt, but the cowboy emerged from this treatment as a "man's man," someone to be taken a bit more seriously than his wild West show and dime-novel image might suggest. With some modifications by Owen Wister the cowboy became the strong, silent character of American popular culture, stout of heart, strong of limb, quick of wit, and endowed with remarkable coordination of hand and eye.

In addition to these qualities, of course, the cowboy is popularly celebrated in song and story for his gentlemanly conduct toward ladies. Not women, mind you, but ladies — for a woman could not be a lady if she earned her living in saloon, dance hall, or brothel.[6] Ladies were hard to find in the West, and therefore they deserved consideration and respect. But the obeisance of literary cowboys aside, there was a prevalent notion that real men were superior, no matter how deferential they might be in the presence of silk and satin. As I have suggested earlier, this superiority became clear in western films, and the mooning cowboy remained a purely literary convention. In films gentlemanly conduct was in reality patronizing regard, and women lost whatever rational edge they had enjoyed in fiction. Indeed, they became even more bland on the printed page, copying their cinematic sisters to the extent that writers of westerns still limned faint-hearted, scatterbrained females long after Theodore Dreiser, Sinclair Lewis, and virtually everyone else in American literature had abandoned such simplemindedness. The cowboy was (Ed Bruce, Waylon Jennings, and others may suggest that he still

[5] Roosevelt got on best with people who shared with him a western background. See William W. Savage, Jr., "Wyoming and the Shaping of a Presidential Adviser: A Comment on Horace Plunkett's Friendship with Theodore Roosevelt," *Annals of Wyoming* 45 (Fall, 1973): 241-48.

[6] See Abbott and Smith, *We Pointed Them North*, chap. 12; and Douglas Branch, *The Cowboy and His Interpreters* (New York: D. Appleton and Company, 1926), p. 151.

is) the proverbial Neanderthal, making his selection from the female population and dragging her back to the cave. But it is important to remember that the choice — to mate or not to mate — was entirely his, and the lady, always hopelessly in love, had not a great deal to say about it.

Roosevelt described the cattle kingdom as a patriarchy, and that aspect of it undoubtedly appealed to him, as did other manly things, like the seeming organization of the roundup along military lines: real men doing men's work, and all that.[7] Cattlemen were patriarchs, after a fashion, and theirs was a man's world. Most of the rest of nineteenth-century America was, too, for that matter; and the circumstances of persons and property at that time, whether eastern or western, lend credence to Kate Millett's theory of sexual politics, according to which sex is a designation of social status.[8] Whatever changes have been wrought in the status of women in the last hundred years, the western as either a literary or cinematic genre, when it deals with the cowboy, has served only to affirm that the woman is as immobile as a bug in amber and that nothing has changed on the fictive frontier.[9]

The woman of cowboy B epics has good instincts, which is to say that she is morally upright in more ways than one, but she is usually not too bright, and she is always helpless. More often than not she has a crotchety father to care for, a beleaguered old geezer whose claim to fame is that he has something (water, land on a railroad right of way, a treasure map) that

[7] Roosevelt, *Ranch Life and the Hunting-Trail*, pp. 6, 53.

[8] Kate Millett, *Sexual Politics* (New York: Avon Books, 1971), chap. 20.

[9] Which is perhaps surprising, in view of the leadership of various western states in establishing the rights of women in law. For an overview see Andrew Sinclair, *The Better Half: The Emancipation of the American Woman* (New York: Harper & Row, 1965). For an idea of what other film genres were doing, see Michael Wood, *America in the Movies* (New York: Basic Books, 1975), chap. 3.

someone else wants. Ordinarily he would be more capable than his daughter, but age has caught up with him — emasculated him, as it were — and he is as helpless as she. If she has no father, then she is probably an eastern do-gooder (journalist, schoolmarm, missionary) who flops around like a fish out of water and discovers trouble in the process. Regardless of what she is or how she got that way, the cowboy hero rides to the rescue, she realizes that he is the man for whom she has waited ever since she was old enough to know she ought to wait, and the story ends with the cowboy having the option of kissing her or his horse. Either she moves from the control of her father into the sphere of cowboy influence or she gives up her career, if not to marry the cowboy then because she at last recognizes her own inadequacy; that is, you have to be a man to get along in a man's world. About the cowboy who chooses his horse or his male companions we shall have more to say later.

The place of women vis-à-vis the cowboy hero adds a new dimension to any discussion of the influence of westerns on American attitudes. We see time and time again the testimony of nostalgic males to the effect that the movie cowboy hero taught manliness, which means that in addition to providing instruction in the arts of fisticuffs and gunslinging he also taught all those little boys how to deal with women.[10] There is evidence to indicate that the cowboy hero merely reinforced juvenile prejudice against women. "When the kids would write me a letter," Roy Rogers has said,

I felt it was my duty to answer 'cause they put a lot of effort into writin' it. Seein' what they said, I more or less gauged myself in the pictures. I tried to improve on their likes, and the dislikes I'd mark out. . . .

[10] See, for example, Buck Rainey, "The 'Reel' Cowboy," in *The Cowboy,* ed. Harris and Rainey, p. 19.

If I looked like I was gonna kiss a girl, I would get a ton of letters from little boys to leave that mushy stuff out 'cause they didn't like it.[11]

So the western marinated sexual immaturity and held it up as a behavioral model for seven decades, if one allows television late shows as an added preservative. This is in keeping with the notion of the film industry, reflecting the view of society at large, that violence is perfectly suitable fare for children but the depiction of mature sexual relationships is not. The difference between a PG rating and an R rating may indeed be the difference between a couple of gallons of synthetic blood and some candid conversation, but it is also the difference between the worlds of fantasy and fact. In adhering to the standard of the B western or looking back fondly upon it, the American male is, like the cowboy hero's woman, an individual in a state of arrested adolescence. Of the several ways to play cowboy, this may be the most unfortunate.

At second glance the cowboy hero's woman was decidedly not an individual. The classy pyrotechnics of a Jean Arthur were perhaps exceptions to the rule, but even she was putty in the virile hands of a William Holden or an Alan Ladd. And besides, she was better than the Bs, unlike Gail Davis, Sheila Terry, Noel Neill, Jane Adams, Lucille Lund, Julia Thayer, Mary Brian, and countless more who were only pretty — and to the audiences nameless — faces. They had more in common, cinematically at least, with the Indians (inasmuch as both were props — flesh and blood, but with the personalities of tables and chairs) than with the cowboy hero or even the heavy, whose characterization was often the most deftly drawn of all.

And cowboys, despite their deference, did not think of these women as individuals either. In the late 1930s, Gene Autry's

---

[11] Morgan, "Conversations with the Cowboy King," p. 18.

name appeared on something called the "Ten Commandments of the Cowboy," a list of dos and don'ts for juveniles that was widely acclaimed as a splendid device of moral instruction. The ninth item began, "A cowboy respects womanhood. . . ."[12] Not women, it said, but womanhood, meaning the state of being a woman or, more impersonally, women collectively. Little boys, then, were to respect any potential wife, child-bearer, or housekeeper, categories of occupation specified in any and all American dictionaries as definitions of the word "woman." The only other segments of the human population designated for respect or kindness were "small children," "old folks," and "parents." A cowboy might be expected to be "free from racial and religious prejudice," but prejudices concerning age and gender warranted itemization. And, in keeping with the cyclical nature of cowboy stereotyping, according to which one thing leads to another and back to the first, Autry and his saddle pals were the ready examples of how to show such respect. B-film women demonstrated what sort of behavior one might expect in return. In Autry's films they rarely got kissed either.

The cowboy hero is symptomatic of a good deal of American confusion over sexuality in general and sex roles in particular, and he deserves study from that perspective no less than, say Hugh Hefner. Each in his own way has been responsible for promoting male fantasies on a vast scale, and each has mis-represented "womanhood" by means of distortion that does not even begin to approach subtlety. What Hefner accomplished with an airbrush and ice cubes, the cowboy hero accomplished by upstaging the ladies with feats of mental and physical agility. Both created a nonwoman, an antiseptic crea-

[12] The list can be found in Richard A. Maynard, *The American West on Film: Myth and Reality* (Rochelle Park, N.J.: Hayden Book Company, 1974), p. 62.

ture without physical blemish who does not communicate and is therefore fantastic, a being in and of another world who is perhaps the result of a mysterious chemical reaction in a five-foot test tube. The very tadpoles who avidly followed the cowboy hero's every adventure are now the equally avid purchasers of *Playboy, Penthouse, Hustler,* and dozens of other unreal publications featuring the same cowboy hero's woman, but this time without her clothes.[13]

In his analysis of certain neurotic elements in western fiction Leslie A. Fiedler has described the literary movement westward as one in which males attempt to escape from their women and to find refuge in a masculine society ensconced in the wilderness. Fiedler's masculine society is based on friendship between white men and Indian men, and while he is more concerned with Cooper's Leatherstocking than with recent manifestations of popular culture, he is describing much that is basic to the cowboy hero as a cinematic convention, if not a literary one. In the fiction women are out to destroy the West by bringing civilization to the wilderness and, like Hannah Duston, chopping up all the Indians.[14] In the films, one imagines, females may be out to destroy the West by recapturing the males who reside therein — by putting an end to their freedom and thereby their individuality. The cowboy hero thus resists the march of civilization by avoiding the clutches of women. Simply put, the cowboy chooses his horse instead of the girl (they are always "girls," never women), or he elects to enjoy the company of his sidekicks; only rarely does he succumb to kissing or marriage.[15] He preserves his freedom, and the West endures.

[13] Consult Frank Brady, *Hefner,* rev. ed. (New York: Ballantine Books, 1975).

[14] Leslie A. Fiedler, *The Return of the Vanishing American* (New York: Stein and Day, 1968), pp. 50-51.

But still they try, these women, to impair the cowboy hero's mobility. That is the nature of women, the films suggest, and their function is to impose domesticity on unwilling males. But the cowboy is a sly fellow, bigger, stronger, and smarter than the female, and no easy prey. And he has another advantage: he is without sexual desire. Consequently, women offer nothing he needs, and certainly nothing worth trading for his freedom.

The historical cowboy, we are told, was sometimes a lusty soul, a patron of whores, and a singer of ribald songs. So is the modern cowboy-drifter, according to his musical chroniclers. But the cowboy hero will have none of that. He is a fighting monk, continent and competent, whose only exertions come from battling for right and whose soul is as white as his hat. It was not until the 1950s that Miss Kitty and the girls at the Longbranch educated America about the cowboy's sexual proclivities, and the subsequent changes in the character of the cowboy hero — his debasement, really — accustomed audiences to the notion that cowboys had glands. The psychopathic cowboys of *The Culpepper Cattle Co.* and Sam Peckinpah's *Pat Garrott and Billy the Kid* (1973) spend much time in the cotes of soiled doves, and if heroes are not of that stripe, then they are like Tom Gries's *Will Penny* (1968), an ignorant cowboy who thinks (but only briefly) of taking a woman only when he is over the hill and halfway into the valley beyond. He is too old, in effect, for anything but sex. The B-film cowboy, however, is involved only with his pals — the theme of the innocent marriage of males, according to literary critics — or with his horse.

The scarcity of women on the frontier of the historical cowboy and the preference of the fictive cowboy for male

15 Branch, *The Cowboy and His Interpreters*, pp. 156-57, speaks to the historical accuracy of the cowboy's single-blessedness.

companionship have raised the specter of cowboy homosexuality in the minds of some observers. Others have suggested that the cowboy is a prime example not of homosexuality but of repressed heterosexuality, since heroics take precedence over the affairs of the heart, loins, or whatever. There is much left to learn about cowboy sexuality, for few historians or novelists have dared to touch the subject.[16] "Men do not cease to be men," William Dale Jennings has rightly noted, "simply because there are no women around. Yet western historians and Hollywood would have us believe that erectile tissue was completely missing in the metabolism of the West."[17]

Another dimension that might be considered is the image of the cowboy hero in America's homosexual subculture. The Rainbow Cattle Company, the Cinch, and the Eagle Creek Saloon are San Francisco bars catering to a clientele of gay cowboys, men who wear western clothes, shoot pool, and listen to country music. It is all a part of something called "gay macho," meaning that effeminate types are not appreciated and everybody is indeed a man's man. H. Ira Klein suggests that many gay cowboys were enamored as children with the image of Roy Rogers. Some concluded that the best way to attract Roy's attention was to be like Dale Evans. Others simply decided to be a masculine companion, a sidekick with whom Roy or some other cowboy hero would ride away after a thrilling adventure. "They don't necessarily want to play with dolls or learn to sew or even listen to Verdi," says

[16] The best treatment is Clifford P. Westermeier, "The Cowboy and Sex," in *The Cowboy*, ed. Harris and Rainey, pp. 85-105. See also David Galloway, "Up Yours, Tonto!" Or, Growing Up Queer in America," in *The Sex Industry*, ed. George Paul Csicsery, (New York: New American Library, 1973), pp. 208-18.

[17] William Dale Jennings, *The Cowboys* (New York: Bantam Books, 1972), pp. 223-24.

Klein. "What they want to do is love their hero and be loved by him."[18]

B-film fantasies led to an almost complete identification of the cowboy hero with the actor who played the part. What the kids at the Saturday matinee did not know was that in real life some of their cowboy heroes showed an inordinate interest in women, as evidenced by their numerous and frequent marriages. Tom Mix led the field with five wives. William Boyd had four, and Hoot Gibson, Don ("Red") Barry, and Tim Holt had three apiece, as did John Wayne. Alan ("Rocky") Lane, Tim McCoy, Audie Murphy, and Randolph Scott were relatively inactive, each marrying only twice. They suggested celibacy while in the saddle, but out of it they were walking testimonials to the promise of connubial bliss.

The concept of family received short shrift in cowboy fantasies as a result of, first, the role assigned to women and, second, the footloose nature of cowboy life. Families, when they existed, were in some sort of trouble (suggesting the weakness of the members either individually or in concert), and the cowboy hero had to set things right (for example, Shane and the Starretts). But sodbuster families are one thing and cowboy families another; and the best-known cowboy family rode the ranges of the Ponderosa on television's "Bonanza" for fourteen years. It is worth noting that the Cartwrights had no women on the spread. The three sons were sired by the same man but were born to three different wives, each of whom had gone to her reward sometime in the distant past. Indeed, the series collapsed after fourteen years only when viewer interest could not be sustained by the notion that the youngest son would finally marry a woman. In its heyday "Bonanza" spawned some imitators, notably "The Big Valley,"

---

[18] H. Ira Klein, "San Francisco's Gay Cowboys," *City* (San Francisco), September 30, 1975, p. 38.

a series about a ranch owned by a woman.[19] It was not a matriarchy but a male oligarchy, and the men did all the hard work, like riding, shooting, and fighting — to say nothing of rescuing the ladies.

There have been attempts at developing cowgirl heroines, but in the B films they were never successful. Gail Davis made eighty-one half-hour episodes of "Annie Oakley" for television in the 1950s, under the auspices of Gene Autry's Flying A Productions. She had a male sidekick named Tagg, and they divided their time pulling each other out of tight spots. The program was meant for kids, so one can only imagine what Annie and her friend did to pass the time when the bad guys were visiting someone else's neighborhood. It was fanciful fare, considering Annie's bizarre costume and her unbelievable trick shots, but here at least was the suggestion of a cowgirl, and the program had some therapeutic value because it made little boys consider the possibility that little girls might be quick on the trigger too. And, well, maybe even quicker, heaven forfend.

There have been only a few Annie Oakleys on the horizon of American entertainment, and certainly no western female rivals Wonder Woman for the adulation of small girls. In the 1940s, Wonder Woman carried almost the whole burden of female heroism, even to the point of traveling through time to set matters aright on the nineteenth-century frontier. In a 1946 episode Wonder Woman encountered Prudence Beene, who might have come straight from a B western, so simple was her trust (to say nothing of her mind) and so complete was her helplessness. Prudence was engaged to Silas Sneek, an employee of her father's, her father being an Indian trader who dressed like a cowboy. Sneek was, naturally, a sneak who got

---

[19] "Lancer" and "The High Chaparral" were other imitators featuring cowboy families with women of low visibility.

the elder Beene in trouble with his customers. Wonder Woman stepped in and, with her magic lasso, made Sneek "fess up," leading Prudence to remark, "I've learned my lesson — I'll rely on *myself, not* on a *man!*"[20] Here was a lady unique in all the West, if the artifacts of popular culture are to be believed.

In the years since World War II the *Virginian's* Molly Wood, Taisie Lockhart of Emerson Hough's *North of 36,* and the sweet young things of the B westerns have been kept alive only by television. Marjorie Rosen has described the excision of women from major films during the 1960s, and as films go, so goes the western.[21] The women who survive on the screen are sybaritic sex objects, and westerns abound with them. With few exceptions the cowboy hero is now a rodeo performer, and because his heroics are less time consuming than those of his two-gun predecessor, he has plenty of idle moments for fun, which is to say sex. He will dally with the ladies for a while, but lasting relationships are no more to his liking than they were to the B-film hero's. So the ladies must be ladies with whom to dally: sexy and agreeable. Sam Peckinpah specializes in this sort of person, and every woman in his films either is a prostitute or acts like one. Whatever the pretension of such films to art, theirs is the stuff of pornography; and pornography takes after the cowboy and his women with great zest and gusto.[22]

Arthur Penn's *The Missouri Breaks* (1976) did introduce a

[20] The episode is reprinted in Gloria Steinem, ed., *Wonder Woman* (New York: Holt, Rinehart and Winston, Warner Books, 1972).

[21] Majorie Rosen, *Popcorn Venus* (New York: Coward, McCann and Geoghegan, 1973), chap. 22. Molly Haskell, *From Reverence to Rape: The Treatment of Women in the Movies* (New York: Holt, Rinehart and Winston, 1974), confirms the diagnosis.

[22] Most of the possibilities are presented in Mullin Garr, *Big Man in the Saddle* (New York: Ophelia Press, 1969); Bret Steele, *Hot Trail* (New York: Midwood Books, 1973); Jeff Bennett, *Loaded Gun* (New York: Carlyle Communications, 1974); and who knows how many others.

new kind of cowgirl to the screen, a rancher's daughter played by Kathleen Lloyd. She is casually courted by Jack Nicholson, a cowboy turned rustler who would like to dally in the best postwar tradition. Lloyd, however, changes the subject. "Why don't we take a walk," she asks Nicholson, "and just talk about the Wild West and how to get the hell out of it." They wind up together, of course, after Nicholson has proved that he, not Marlon Brando — the psychopathic bounty hunter hired by the rancher to rid the range of rustlers — should wear the white hat. There are many of the usual neowestern conventions here — lynching, shooting, cutting, cursing, and so forth — but Lloyd bears up with the best view of life that could be sustained in all that turmoil, and she struggles through without any of the histrionics characteristic of her cinematic ancestors. Here is the match that the cowboy hero has long needed, but whether or not her kind will reappear regularly is still in doubt. The man's man, and the men who enjoy watching him, may not tolerate the intrusion.[23] This sort of woman may not be too hot to handle, but it is certain that she will be smart enough to know what is going on.

[23] Such intolerance is the subject of Joan Mellen, *Big Bad Wolves: Masculinity in the American Film* (New York: Pantheon Books, 1977).

·7·
Salesmanship

THE COWBOY HERO has always been a commodity. He may be part of a mythic construct of America's past, and his image in popular culture may be rife with sociological and psychological implications, but he exists in the first place because of a superior act of marketing. In the last quarter of the nineteenth century the cowboy hero was manufactured and sold to the American public in a manner similar to that employed in the manufacture and sale of any other product of the industrial revolution. He resulted from the efforts of men working in the best American entrepreneurial tradition of making something from nothing.

There was no cowboy hero before William F. Cody presented William Levi Taylor, aka "Buck" Taylor, to the public as a featured attraction in his wild West pageant in 1884. The handsome young Taylor was a cowboy — and a Texan at that — who had worked on Cody's ranch in Nebraska, but that was hardly sufficient reason to offer him for popular consumption. In fact, there was no reason at all for his debut except Cody's desire to find something new with which to entertain eastern audiences. Cody had already exploited virtually every western type in his relatively new but much-traveled show, and it may have been that the cowboy was simply the bottom of the barrel, the last item left to sell. In the 1880s the cowboy had an unsavory reputation, owing to the prevalence of published reports concerning his tacky appearance, his violent behavior, and his disregard for the peace and quiet of Sunday mornings, church socials, and family picnics. For every Roosevelt who sang his praises there were a dozen journalists to damn his bad manners, and not a few of his critics were the cattlemen who employed him.[1] In all he was not the sort of person one would take one's children to see; he was, rather, a pernicious influence best avoided by responsible parents. So Cody had no easy chore to make Buck Taylor palatable, but he did it, and the salesmanship was something for any entrepreneur to envy.

Taylor was, said Cody, "a typical Westerner by ancestry, birth and heritage of association."[2] That led Cody to the subject of antecedents, for he knew the importance of family as a selling point. According to Cody's literature, Taylor came from a long line of decent folk: a grandfather and an uncle died at the Alamo, other relatives fought with Houston at San Jacinto, and his father (a cavalryman) died during the Civil War — splendid credentials in an imperialistic age. Moreover, Taylor was orphaned in his eighth year, and Cody suggested that he was lucky to have grown up at all. He became a cowboy because that was what one did in postwar Texas, and in the process of cowboying he developed "sturdy qualities" necessary to cope with "a daily life . . . replete with privations, hardship, and danger," to say nothing of "excitements and adventures."[3] He was some shakes as a cowhand — so much so, in

[1] Joseph G. McCoy, *Historic Sketches of the Cattle Trade of the West and Southwest* (Kansas City, Mo.: Ramsey, Millett & Hudson, 1874), chap. 8; Gressley, *Bankers and Cattlemen*, p. 125.

[2] Program, Cody's Wild West (1888), p. 28.

[3] Ibid.

fact, that one might take him to be the foremost cowboy in the West and other diverse parts. Cody spoke frequently of Taylor's size and physical strength — he stood over six foot three and could throw steers and break wild horses — and of his "remarkable dexterity." Yet withal he had "genial qualities" and was as "amiable as a child."[4] Promotional photographs were carefully staged to portray Taylor as handsome and harmless and were a further encouragement to cautious parents or apprehensive spectators. Taylor became a hit.

But Cody was not finished. If he could market Taylor in person, the job could be done in print as well, and that aspect of the promotion fell to Prentiss Ingraham, Cody's friend and biographer and a prolific writer of dime novels. In 1887, Ingraham published *Buck Taylor, King of the Cowboys; or, The Raiders and the Rangers: A Story of the Wild and Thrilling Life of William L. Taylor* in Beadle's Half-Dime Library and gave the cowboy hero his literary origin, reinforcing interest in the real article, which could be seen for the price of a ticket to Cody's Wild West.[5]

Cody and Ingraham were packaging entertainment. Most of it was designed for children, and the children were receptive. The extent of their reverence for Buck Taylor was revealed by showman Dexter W. Fellows in his autobiography when he recalled a visit by Cody's show to Fitchburg, Massachusetts. Fellows was a young boy, and he and some pals were watching the touring company board a train when suddenly some bison

[4] Ibid.

[5] Albert Johannsen, *The House of Beadle and Adams and Its Dime and Nickel Novels: The Story of a Vanished Literature* (Norman: University of Oklahoma Press, 1950) 1:277. The exact date of publication was February 1, 1887. Cody's management of Taylor's career is discussed in Henry Nash Smith, *Virgin Land: The American West as Symbol and Myth* (Cambridge, Mass.: Harvard University Press, 1950), chap. 9; and Don Russell, *The Lives and Legends of Buffalo Bill,* 3d printing (Norman: University of Oklahoma Press, 1969), pp. 305-306.

rebelled at efforts to load them into a cattle car. Buck Taylor was there, and he asked Fellows to hold his horse's reins while he supervised moving the bison. "For fifteen minutes," wrote Fellows,

I held Buck Taylor's horse. For me it was a quarter of an hour of glory. There I stood in a circle of kids who begged me to let them hold the reins for just a minute. I clung to them blissfully until their owner returned, patted me on the head, and rode off to the train. For weeks afterward I basked in the reputation of the boy who held the horse for the "King of the Cowboys."[6]

Thousands upon thousands of boys in generations to come would share Fellows's fixation and would, not coincidentally, spend millions of grubby pennies to catch a glimpse of their own particular cowboy hero or, better yet, to purchase something with his name on it.

Cody, of course, never dreamed of the sales potential of the cowboy image. That discovery was made by entrepreneurs of a later day, and once it became known, the thread of cowboy imagery was woven inextricably into the fabric of American business, and near its most durable fiber, American advertising.

The thought of the cowboy as merchandise or as a merchandising device is undoubtedly abhorrent to some, but the evidence speaks for itself. Just as the historical cowboy is a problem in economic history, so the fictive cowboy hero is a problem in entrepreneurial history, and to a greater extent than has been generally understood. Money resides with the cowboy image, and wherever that image appears, one may be certain that profit lurks in the vicinity. The cowboy hero has not the solemnity of art, but rather he is mired in the finan-

[6] Dexter W. Fellows and Andrew A. Freeman, *This Way to the Big Show: The Life of Dexter Fellows* (New York: Viking Press, 1936), p. 36.

cial aspirations of his creators. Why write fiction except to sell? Why make a film except to charge admissions? Why paint? Why sculpture? Certainly there is a creative drive to be satisfied, but satisfaction does not pay bills or buy food, and the creative person with no other source of income who is content to shape his art only for himself is probably, in these last years of the twentieth century, a half-starved loony whose work is not very good anyway. And if he is not and if his work is decent, chances are he has been corrupted by the dollar and plies his craft with the market in mind. Western art, to which countless galleries and whole museums are devoted, is really a variety of commercial art, tremendously popular but descended more from the pictorial journalism of Remington than from any fine tradition of painting and sculpture. And as any gallery owner will tell you, there is money to be made in it.[7]

Marketing made the cowboy hero a gunslinger and gave him beautiful women with whom to contend, because the cowboy could not be portrayed accurately and interestingly at the same time. The historical cowboy may not have been plain, but his work certainly limited his dramatic possibilities. Violence and the suggestion of sex changed all that, making the cowboy at least as interesting as the detective, another nineteenth-century fabrication with a dime-novel adolescence, if a more literate genesis. The cowboy hero was,

[7] See Ron Butler, "The Big Boom in Western Art," *Arizona Highways*, March, 1972, pp. 40-44; and Glen Bayless, "Up From Calendars," *Sunday Oklahoman* (Oklahoma City), November 19, 1972. The cowboy's place in all of this is demonstrated in Ed Ainsworth, *The Cowboy in Art* (New York: World Publishing Company, 1968); John Meigs, ed., *The Cowboy in American Prints* (Chicago: Swallow Press, 1972); and the entire October, 1970, issue of *Arizona Highways*. Representative published collections include Joe Beeler, *Cowboys and Indians: Characters in Oil and Bronze* (Norman: University of Oklahoma Press, 1967); and Louise Phippen, ed., *The Life of a Cowboy: Told Through the Drawings, Paintings, and Bronzes of George Phippen* (Tucson: University of Arizona Press, 1969).

however, still hindered by the limitations of time and place, and regardless of the attempts to make him contemporary, he was ill-suited for fictive life outside the nineteenth century. But guns and women sustain interest even yet, and the cowboy hero finds himself ever farther removed from the cattle that were his raison d'être. That is a necessary circumstance if entrepreneurs of the cowboy hero are to show a profit.

In the marketing milieu of the twentieth century the cowboy hero has acquired impressive credentials as a salesman. Established as a desirable commodity in his own right, the cowboy hero saw his image associated with other products by entrepreneurs wishing to enhance the appeal of those products. The cowboy hero "endorsed" many items that had nothing to do with cowboys and would have been out of place in anybody's West. Beginning in the 1930s, for example, wristwatches were a hot item for cowboy salesmen, and Tom Mix, Gene Autry, and Roy Rogers sold millions of them, along with pocket watches and alarm clocks. U.S. Time Corporation's Hopalong Cassidy wristwatch, first marketed in 1950, came mounted on a miniature saddle and packed in a box printed to resemble a log cabin. There was also a message from Hoppy informing children of the importance of time and encouraging them to be punctual. The watch was intended, said the blurb, to be "a means of bringing you great joy, happiness and success by keeping track of every minute of every hour."[8] Ingraham's 1951 Roy Rogers wristwatch featured more potent cowboy imagery. It had a leather strap that was "Pliable as a lariat, Tough as a Bronco," and fitted with a "Texas-type buckle and tip."[9] Purchasers of this timepiece received a ninety-day guarantee and a wholly superfluous deputy's badge.

[8] Robert Lesser, *A Celebration of Comic Art and Memorabilia* (New York: Hawthorn Books, 1975), p. 130.
[9] Ibid., p. 160.

The image of the cowboy hero was exploited in more complex merchandizing schemes as well. Ralston Purina, the Saint Louis cereal company, sponsored the varied adventures of Tom Mix on radio from 1933 to 1938 and from 1940 to 1950 and all the while peddled tons of tin, wood, and plastic premiums to listeners, each item usually going for a thin dime and a Ralston box top. Premiums included toy guns, compasses, magnifying glasses, rings, bracelets, plastic arrowheads, buttons, and medals. The cowboy sold the cereal, the cereal was necessary to acquire the premium, and the premium reinforced interest in the cowboy, which meant, presumably, more listening and more eating and of course more dimes. As its contribution to cowboy imagery, Ralston Purina merely repeated the outrageous lies of the Hollywood publicists, who made Tom Mix the most fictitious man who ever lived. The company's commitment to profit was reflected in the continuation of the program for a decade after Tom Mix's death and the availability of the premiums for at least two years after the program ended.[10]

Merchandise endorsement made the cowboy hero an expert. Of the many things he knew, he knew especially what was good to eat, and cereal companies made hay — or sold it? — under his auspices. The historical cowboy, as Joseph McCoy said, was the very picture of malnutrition, but the cowboy hero might well have held a degree in home economics, so

---

[10] John Dunning, *Tune in Yesterday: The Ultimate Encyclopedia of Old-Time Radio, 1925-1976* (Englewood Cliffs, N.J.: Prentice-Hall, 1976), pp. 609-11; *Jim Harmon's Nostalgia Catalogue* (Los Angeles: J. P. Tarcher, 1973), pp. 8-25. On the selling of Tom Mix see Paul E. Mix, *The Life and Legend of Tom Mix* (New York: A. S. Barnes and Company, 1972). That Mix was a natural to plug Purina is suggested by the sketch of the company's founder, William H. Danforth, in Sterling G. Slappey, comp., *Pioneers of American Business* (New York: Grosset & Dunlap, 1973), pp. 234-39.

ardent was his praise of brand-name foodstuff.[11] On radio Roy Rogers (Quaker Oats), Sky King (Peter Pan), Red Ryder (Langendorf Bread), Hopalong Cassidy (General Mills), and Buck Jones (Grape Nuts Flakes) were quick-food gourmets with an interest in building good muscles, teeth, and bones.[12] Skeptics who questioned the nutritional value of Ralston Wheat Cereal were invited to "ask Tom Mix; he'll tell you," which ought to be enough information for anybody.[13] The efficacy of such advertising was demonstrated again and again by sales figures, and three decades after Mix could no longer answer questions, readers of cereal boxes might still encounter rhetoric such as this, from the side panel of a package of sugar-coated cereal: "Cowboys learned a long time ago, that to be up at the crack of dawn working hard till noon, it took a good-sized balanced breakfast. We couldn't agree more."[14]

As time passed, the cowboy became less an authority on products and more a symbol whose function was to attract the consumer's attention, to make the potential customer pay attention before paying cash. Television made it easy to use anonymous cowboys, whereas radio had required name identification of heroes before the endorsement could proceed. Television ads were situational — they were sixty-second dramas — and therefore versatile, allowing manufacturers to use any symbol they wished. Still they used the cowboy, owing to his high visibility as a character. In a certain cough drop ad, for example, a cowboy coughs and starts a stampede. He is anonymous, but one need not know who he is, because it is

[11] McCoy, *Historic Sketches*, pp. 137-38.

[12] Dunning, *Tune in Yesterday*, pp. 287, 290, 506, 526, 557.

[13] Liner notes, *Tom Mix: Original Radio Broadcasts* (Mark 56 Records 596).

[14] In 1977, the manufacturer redesigned the cereal package, replacing a photograph of a working cowboy with a cartoon cowboy named Big Yella and omitting any statement about cowboy knowledge of nutrition.

perfectly clear what he is. He functions to call attention to a situation, not to endorse a product, for who today need purchase cough medicine to avoid causing stampedes? Similarly, Red Ryder Shock Absorbers have nothing to do with the hero whose name they bear, and a simple western landscape is enough to attract attention. "America's famous fighting cowboy" (as Red was known on radio) does not put in an appearance, nor is there anything besides the name to suggest his existence.

Cowboy gimmickry found no better application in television commercials than with the use of impersonators of John Wayne to push and such products as pickup trucks and oil filters. Here the intent was humorous: to lampoon the Wayne image and, in the process, to draw attention to the product. But Wayne's image is not to be taken lightly, and impersonators are a lot less interesting than the real thing. Coming late to television, Wayne was the voice of authority in 1975 when, in cowboy garb, he sold United States Savings Bonds in the name of patriotism and the forthcoming Bicentennial, and again in 1977, when, also in cowboy garb, he *told* the American people to take Datril 500 for their headaches. The impersonators ran for cover.

The best example of product identification with the cowboy — indeed, the classic example of product identification with anything — is demonstrated in the advertising for a brand of cigarettes, which has to do with an anonymous cowboy known throughout the world as the Marlboro Man. His story is well known: how he met the advertiser's need for a strong masculine image to sell to male smokers a product once intended for women and how he supplanted all other masculine types with a forcefulness that enabled the company to abandon the symbolic tattoo that had adorned its previous macho models. And much has been made of his meaning — perhaps too much. Bruce A. Lohof, for example, has suggested that the Marlboro

Man is "not simply a cowboy. He is a symbol of irretrievable innocence," and, more, he may well be a manifestation of that good old American Adam that R. W. B. Lewis invented for the amusement of professors of literature.[15]

On television the commercials presented assorted minutes of working cowboy life. The Marlboro Man had plenty to do, looking after horses and cattle, riding through deep snow, and so forth. Regardless of the activity, he would need a smoke, of course, and while he puffed and looked rugged, the audience would be encouraged to "come to Marlboro County," where the flavor was. The Marlboro Man himself never said a word, but the complex message was clear: you came to Marlboro Country by smoking Marlboros, and since the trip took place in your head anyway, while you were at it you might as well pretend you were a cowboy. When the last television commercial ran in September, 1970, the narrator could state with some certainty, "Today, the West is everywhere." Indeed it was, for by then the Marlboro landscape conformed perfectly to the convolutions of the viewer's brain, with all that such conformity implied.

Marlboro continued to present its cowboy and its landscape to confirmed and potential smokers in magazine advertisements after 1970. The photographs were impressive: they had a dramatic impact that was simultaneously nostalgic and immediate, and always the cowboy was at the forefront.[16] One might wonder exactly what Marlboro was selling — cigarettes?

[15] Bruce A. Lohof, "The Higher Meaning of Marlboro Cigarettes," in *Side-Saddle on the Golden Calf: Social Structure and Popular Culture in America*, ed. George H. Lewis (Pacific Palisades, Calif.: Goodyear Publishing Company, 1972), p. 31.

[16] As it happened, the Marlboro Man really was a cowboy. See Mason Smith, "The Marlboro Man," *Sports Illustrated*, January 17, 1977, pp. 58-67.

an image? escape? — and the questions became more pointed when the company occasionally offered nontobacco products to its public. In 1975, for example, Marlboro offered smokers a range jacket, an article of cowboy clothing made of prefaded denim and wool-lined for "hard work and raw weather on the open range."[17] Again the message was clear: if you come to Marlboro Country, you ought to dress the part. These jackets — one was pictured in the advertisement — looked faded, wrinkled, and worn. They looked old enough to be good, with just the right flavor for going where the flavor was.[18]

In prime time in the 1970s cowboys sold barbecue-flavor potato chips for Frito-Lay, motor oil for Phillips 66, trucks for Toyota, and beer for Miller and Schlitz. They sold bath soap, cigars, juice, razors, snuff, barbecue sauce, flashlight batteries, and laundry detergent. They sold just about everything under the sun. The interesting thing about the commercials was not the way the cowboy image was linked to unlikely products but rather the presentation of characteristics assumed to be (and evidently accepted as) typically cowboy. Falstaff Beer went completely to cowboy imagery in 1972 and stayed there for several months, presenting to viewers a series of commercials depicting two modern cowboys at work and play. These jovial saddle pals cavorted in the snow, took the truck to town to pick up a load of feed, raced their horses, and went to the store to see some girls. In each vignette they exhibited behavior that can only be termed adolescent and

[17] Advertisement, *Psychology Today,* February, 1975, p. 13.

[18] The trail driver's shirt that Marlboro advertised in 1977 looked newer, but it was "as rugged as a cowboy's job" and promised to keep "the weather off a man." *Time,* September 19, 1977, p. 27. The shirt and the range jacket were only two of many items offered for sale by Marlboro. At one time the company even issued a "chuckwagon cookbook" containing recipes for "great foods that capture all the flavor of Marlboro Country."

demonstrated a marked preference for raising hell to working hard or, indeed, working at all. Viewers were extended an invitation to have some Falstaff and join the fun. Referring, no doubt, to life in general, the announcement said, "We're all in this together" (and certainly we are, since the West is everywhere).

Richard Dorson's suggestions for the analysis of cowboy songs might well be applied to cowboy commercials as a measure of the popular mind and its perceptions of the cowboy. What do we learn about him? The Falstaff advertisements tell us that in his contemporary manifestations he is little more than a kid. Dash detergent, on the other hand, argues that he is a hard worker in a dirty job: "Now, if Dash can get thirteen cowboys' shirts clean, think what it can do on your dirty clothes." And an aftershave says that he is a sexy thing who only pretends to want to escape from women, when in reality he would prefer to be caught by the blonde beauties who are inclined to pursue him. In no instance is the cowboy of the commercials akin to the B-film hero; the only similarity is in clothing style. The composite commercial cowboy is a grubby adolescent sex object, the antithesis of the movie hero but closer, except for the sex, to the historical cowboy.

As any effective salesman tries to be, the cowboy in advertising is all things to all people. That is a difficult job of work, and of all American characters only the cowboy could be up to it. Of the various uses to which the cowboy has been put, however, this is the most destructive, because advertising fractures the image of the cowboy and presents the bits and pieces to the undivided attention of large numbers of people. And this is the way the cowboy is most often seen in the last quarter of the twentieth century, for in the absence of pulp fiction, B films, radio dramas, and television programs, advertising is his medium and the vehicle that contributes most to the presentation of his image to mass audiences.

Advertising points to the dichotomy concerning heroes in the American mind. No matter how much the American people revere their heroes or tout their myths, they will sell them all to any buyer and at nearly any price. The sale of heroes, and thereby the sale of national myths, is a uniquely American phenomenon, and it can result in the debasement of myth and the destruction of tradition.[19] Commercial exploitation of the cowboy has always been largely responsible for the tacky tinsel aspects of his image, and that, in turn, speaks to the frequent shallowness of American culture and its poverty of myth. The whole thrust of American history has been toward discounting that which cannot be sold and ennobling that which can.[20] Thus cultural significance depends upon marketability, and the cowboy derives most of his importance from his appeal as an article of merchandise. The cowboy is a prime example of the relationship between culture and cash in the United States, inasmuch as his image is sold with equal

[19] Skeptics are invited to reconsider the Bicentennial, an event memorable for its souvenirs and salesmanship.

[20] Again, skeptics are invited to watch an evening of commercial television. Those who are not up to having the experience first hand may wish to peruse the following titles: Gaye Tuchman, ed., *The TV Establishment: Programming for Power and Profit* (Englewood Cliffs, N.J.: Prentice-Hall, 1974); Charles Sopkin, *Seven Glorious Days, Seven Fun-filled Nights* (New York: Simon & Schuster, 1968); Michael J. Arlen, *The View from Highway 1* (New York: Farrar, Straus and Giroux, 1976); Harlan Ellison, *The Glass Teat: Essays of Opinion on the Subject of Television* (New York: Pyramid Books, 1975); and Harlan Ellison, *The Other Glass Teat: Further Essays of Opinion on Television* (New York: Pyramid Books, 1975). On the impact of electronic media see (in addition to McLuhan) Edmund Carpenter, *Oh, What a Blow That Phantom Gave Me!* (New York: Holt, Rinehart and Winston, 1973). For a discussion of the manufacture of culture see Wilson Bryan Key, *Media Sexploitation* (Englewood Cliffs, N.J.: Prentice-Hall, 1976), especially chap. 12. On the subject of television advertising see Terry Galanoy, *Down the Tube* (New York: Pinnacle Books, 1972).

energy by those who take him seriously and by those who do not. Continued emphatic exploitation might stand to prevent the development of the cowboy as an aspect of socially useful myth by saddling him with the restrictive identity of merchandise, were it not manifestly clear that he has grown accustomed to his chores.

·8·
Athletics

THE RODEO PERFORMER is a contrivance of the twentieth century, and the promoters responsible for his keep would have it believed that he is a cowboy. But he is not. Rodeo is a major spectator sport, like football, baseball, basketball, or ice hockey, and the individual who participates in it is an athlete. If that is not a common perception, it is perhaps because rodeo contains too many variables to permit liberal placement of sixty-second commercials and has therefore had little impact upon television markets. Rodeo is, nevertheless, an enormously popular sport, and, like soccer, it grows in popularity each year with only minimal television exposure. Several of its performers, on the basis of their earnings alone, can be considered to be superstars. They extend the cowboy image, but they are not cowboys, a condition shared with many others, as we have seen.

Originally, rodeo (the word comes from the Spanish verb *rodear,* meaning, in Central and South America, *"to round up")* was a pastime for cowboys. The name rodeo was not applied to the sport until the twentieth century, but the contests were prevalent in the nineteenth-century West and afforded cowboys the opportunity to compete among themselves in demonstrating the skills by which they earned their living. By the 1880s the competition was more formalized, and a number of western communities featured contests pitting cowboys from one ranch against cowboys from another. There was thus a team aspect to early rodeos, wherein cowboys strove to distinguish themselves for the honor of the old Hash Knife, Rocking R, or whatever. At this point rodeo became more than a diversion or mere recreation.[1]

The various traveling shows that presented the West to eastern audiences at the turn of the century fostered popular interest in cowboy skills (such as they were) and added the element of exhibitionism that characterizes modern rodeo. The team aspect disappeared, and the emerging sport became a showcase for individual ability.

As the twentieth century progressed, cowboy skills became less important as prerequisites for employment in the workaday world. They were of paramount importance, however, in the rodeo arena, where money might be made. These circumstances led to increased specialization by performers, who were, after all, being paid for what they could do, and the better they did it the better they were paid. Rodeo cowboys began doing things that working cowboys seldom considered — bulldogging, for example, had little practical application to western ranching practices — and all to enhance their appeal to paying customers. The premise was (and is) that rodeo preserved and perpetuated cowboy skills, when, in fact, it did (and does) not. But to a public blissfully unaware of the reality of cowboy life, rodeo was the genuine article. Building

---

[1] V. H. Whitlock, *Cowboy Life on the Llano Estacado* (Norman: University of Oklahoma Press, 1970), chap. 21. The best general introduction to rodeo is still Clifford P. Westermeier, *Man, Beast, Dust: The Story of Rodeo* (Denver: World Press, 1947).

upon this, rodeo's exponents could proclaim it to be the last vital link with our frontier past, and they could speak of "the living legend of the cowboy."[2]

Certainly the rodeo performer perceives of himself as a cowboy, but that is not a perception shared by many modern ranch hands. Journalist Bill Surface discovered in 1972 that most of the men he interviewed for his report on the contemporary working cowboy had never heard of fellow-Texan Phil Lyne, the Rodeo Cowboys' Association's "All Around Champion" in 1971. And they knew as little about Larry Mahan, perhaps the most renowned rodeo performer of the 1960s and 1970s. Surface observed, in addition, the antipathy of one foreman who condemned rodeo as a financial attraction that removed from the range promising young men who, in time, might actually have learned something about cowboying. Surface found that most of his informants had competed in rodeos at one time or another but that none of them had taken it seriously as a money-making proposition. All agreed that rodeo performers were hardly cowboys.[3]

The Rodeo Cowboys' Association, first established as the Cowboys' Turtle Association in 1936, is a major-league organization for professionals, and there are other, though

[2] Christopher Lofting, "Editorial," *Rodeo*, September-October, 1971, p. 3. Similarly, there is the 1974 documentary film about rodeo, *The Great American Cowboy*, advertised by American National Enterprises, Inc., as the "exciting true story of a vanishing american [*sic*] and his special kind of freedom." A historical connection is further suggested by the establishment of the National Rodeo Hall of Fame as a part of the National Cowboy Hall of Fame and Western Heritage Center. Finally, there are such items as country singer Red Steagall's 1977 album *For All Our Cowboy Friends* (ABC-Dot Do 2078), a collection of songs about rodeo performers. The liner notes speak of the spirit of the American West and how rodeo cowboys preserve it.

[3] Surface, *Roundup at the Double Diamond*, pp. 24, 148. Consider also the various opinions throughout Jane Kramer, *The Last Cowboy* (New York: Harper & Row, 1977).

smaller, professional rodeo groups. And, as is the case with professional football or baseball, there are college leagues and minor leagues. There are even little-league rodeo associations for small fry. The International Rodeo Association sponsors the Miss Rodeo USA Pageant in conjunction with its championship events, which is but one example of the entrepreneurial activity attendant upon what may be characterized as the rodeo industry. The pages of rodeo magazines carry advertisements for stock contractors and rodeo producers, clowns, announcers, variety acts, promotion specialists, booking agents, photographers, clothing, equipment, ticket companies, and trophies. Rodeo Sports Therapy, of Simonton, Texas, markets tape, bandages, linament, vitamins, salt tablets, and other medical paraphernalia specifically for rodeo performers. And so forth. The big leagues mean big business in other sports. Thus it is with rodeo.

"Rodeo," Gerald C. Lubenow has observed, "is an incredibly heavy male trip."[4] And it is one for which the child prepares at a remarkably tender age in the rural West. The effects of little-league sport upon children have, of course, received national attention in recent years, but as yet no one has offered anything of even *The Bad News Bears* genre of exposé about peewee rodeo and its nascent machismo.[5] Nor is anyone likely to do so, for the reason that few urbanites, or indeed anyone on the east bank of the Mississippi River, would believe it.

And kiddie rodeo must be seen to be believed. On the one hand, it may simply be taken (like some other sports) as an example of what Lewis H. Lapham has called "the American grudge against children."[6] On the other hand, it may represent

[4] Gerald C. Lubenow, "Rodeo: The Soul of the Frontier," *Newsweek,* October 2, 1972, p. 27.

[5] See, for example, James A. Michener, *Sports in America* (New York: Random House, 1976), chap. 4.

an atavistic response to modernity, a harking back to those frontier days when every male human being experienced a rite of passage wherein he actually risked a broken neck. Medically, the particulars may be forborne, but their psychological consequences require scrutiny, given the larger context of cowboy imagery.

Consider for a moment the boy who is taught to ride a horse in his second year, who is placed aboard bucking stock at four, who is graduated to bull riding at five (by which time he has learned to chew tobacco and swear), and who, by the age of eight, has sustained at least one serious injury and probably more. He is supported and encouraged to do these things by his parents, his siblings, and his peers. He considers himself to be a cowboy and affects the dress and speech of one.[7] His maturity may be measured by the rapidity with which he passes from Happy Days mint or raspberry to the full-bodied flavor of Copenhagen or Skoal.

This boy — who is all too typical in the rural West — competes in a sport from which females are barred (that is, in all events except barrel racing and pole racing — themselves sufficiently dangerous to fetch young ladies a crack on the noggin or a couple of broken ribs), and the atmosphere in which he performs has much in common with that generated by Hollywood for the B-film cowboy hero. Which is to say that the little fellow gets a good deal of admiration from small girls, who already know their place. The experience is surely instructive, consisting as it does of the stuff from which men are made. Females thus join danger, competition, and tobacco upon the periodic table of the elements of life.

[6] Lewis H. Lapham, "Hostages to Fortune," *Harper's*, April, 1978, p. 12.

[7] See Bob Colvin, "A Cowboy's Life Is Tough," *Orbit Magazine, Sunday Oklahoman* (Oklahoma City), November 4, 1973.

Kiddie rodeo, like other little-league sports, exists rather more for the sake of the parents than for the children, and the aberrant behavior of the parental fan is much in evidence in the stands. Parents critically evaluate each child's performance, and whether or not he is their offspring or someone else's is irrelevant. They are blunt and vocal, and often they are merciless in confronting the inept child. That child, moreover, has no place to hide. No face guard obscures his features, and no number on a uniform disguises his identity. Most of the community may be present, and he is known to all. It is expected that he will act like a man, no matter how grievous his tactical error coming out of the chute and no matter how painful his injuries. And, despite his years, he acts like a man, or at least in ways he has learned to believe are manly. He has learned well in the dust and dung of the arena. He must not be sick from chewing tobacco. He must never cry. Cowboys do not cry.[8]

Nor, in American popular culture, do they show much emotion of any kind, except perhaps toward their horses. Little-league rodeo teaches one to avoid even that, inasmuch as it encourages flagrant cruelty to animals. Barrel racers are told by adults to beat their horses on the head, and beat them hard, until they learn to turn in the required direction at the appropriate time. Bucking stock is often so jaded by incessant riding that it is not bucking stock at all, having been broken to saddle or rope many times over. Consequently, broncs and bulls must be motivated to perform by men wielding electric cattle prods. Often a child's ride is preceded by as much as five minutes' worth of such motivation, so that the animal

---

[8] I admit to having seen a young rodeo performer cry once, after his horse introduced him to a fence post in a small-town arena. The boy cried, but no adult would examine his injury or even console him — until he stopped.

leaves the chute in a wild-eyed frenzy of fear and pain, all the better, in the adult view, for scoring points. One does not win, after all, without scoring points.

There is greater scrutiny of rodeo at the professional level, and the possibility of such abuses is minimized. But the violence remains — the violence of the encounter between man and the untamed animal — because it is basic to the sport, of course, and also because it is basic to the image of the cowboy hero. Bad men and bad broncs are all the same to the hero, for they exist only to be subdued in manly fashion. Thus the rodeo performer, in the violence of his endeavor, is akin to the cowboy hero from whom he acquires his image and perhaps even his view of the relationships of life.

Rodeo confirms the image of the cowboy as a tough, masculine character in the popular mind. Television employs rodeo performers to sell products in which — and on this point the messages are clear — no sissy would dare to traffic, for example, smokeless tobacco and low-calorie beer. Presumably the chubby spectator will then feel no fear of embarrassment at opting for a six-pack of "lite" at the neighborhood grocery, in full view of his tattooed ex Marine confreres, and even if he does, he can easily prove his grit by packing his jaw with a quid of Walt Garrison's favorite pastime.[9] Cowboys, though not necessarily rodeo performers, also peddle chewing gum to those who cannot abide even a small pinch between cheek and gum but would like to feel manly nevertheless. The watchword here is masculine, because, as with other manifestations of the image, being a cowboy means meaning business.

In diametrical opposition to this, however, is the treatment

---

[9] Garrison, a football player and rodeo performer — a Dallas Cowboy cowboy, as it were — achieved minor fame in television commercials in the early 1970's by observing, of his wintergreen-flavored Skoal, "Feels real relaxin' in there."

accorded the rodeo performer in fiction and film — treatment suggesting that the rodeo performer is one, and perhaps the foremost, of life's losers. The heroic status of the cowboy is simply not extended wholesale to the rodeo performer, a contemporary character who comes off in entertainment media as an individual who struggles less against the beasts than against himself. Films ranging across two decades, from Budd Boetticher's *Bronco Buster* (1952) and Nicholas Ray's *The Lusty Men* (1952) to Peckinpah's *Junior Bonner,* Cliff Robertson's *J. W. Coop,* Stuart Millar's *When the Legends Die,* and Steve Ihnat's *The Honkers* (all 1972), variously portray rodeo performers as puerile, petulant, shallow, egocentric, often violent, and almost always self-destructive men who are heroic for perhaps no more than fifteen seconds at a time and whose relationships with other human beings (especially female human beings) are generally defective. Typical is the character played by Montgomery Clift in John Huston's *The Misfits* (1961). He is aptly described by the film's title, and he is a sympathetic character precisely because he is a misfit, a soft-spoken failure who lies to his mother in long-distance telephone accounts of his nonexistent victories in the rodeo arena. Inasmuch as his life is devoid of major affective relationships and empty of all but the most trivial ambitions, and inasmuch as he remains unaware of his personal and professional limitations, he is the archetypal cinematic rodeo performer. Simply put, he is addicted to rodeo in the same way that an alcoholic is addicted to drink, and with the same results: physical and psychological deterioration, isolation, and so forth. Indeed, he is portrayed as having much in common with a wino. He may once have known how to overcome his addiction, but he lacked the will, and, after a certain point, he lost the desire.

The character is replayed in popular fiction. Occasional variations allow the rodeo performer to emerge as a family man who exhibits at least a smattering of middle-class values or

to become, after a successful rodeo career, something else —
perhaps even a hero.[10] Yet, withal, the rodeo performer is a
character with marginal dramatic potential, and attempts to
portray him heroically are infrequent and short-lived. Witness,
for example, television's "Stoney Burke" (ABC) and "The
Wide Country" (NBC), series, which aired during 1962. Both
featured rodeo performers as protagonists, and both survived
but a single season. The 1960s was the zenith decade of the
television western, but while the rodeo format afforded the
sorts of dramatic possibilities (weekly changes of locale and
population, for example) that had ensured the success of
dozens of western programs, it seems clear that rodeo performers paled in comparison to the "genuine" television cowboy heroes of "Rawhide" (1959-65), "The Virginian" (1962-
70) or "Bonanza" (1959-73), men of remarkable longevity.
From another perspective one might add that there has been a
paucity of successful television dramatic series about athletes
of any variety.[11]

If the cowboy image is central to rodeo, it is also more than
peripheral to some other professional sports. Cowboy imagery
was prominently displayed in January, 1978, during the festiv-

[10] William Crawford, *The Bronc Rider* (New York: G. P. Putnam's
Sons, 1965); and Aaron Fletcher, *Cowboy* (New York: Belmont Tower
Books, 1977), depict the seamy side of things, while Herbert Harker,
Goldenrod (New York: Random House, 1972), holds out hope, if not for
the sport, then for the people in it. John Reese, *Omar, Fats and Trixie*
(Greenwich, Conn.: Fawcett Publications, 1976), tells about a stove-up
rodeo performer who becomes a detective.
[11] "The Busters," a horrid sixty-minute CBS pilot shown in May, 1978,
did not promise to change the situation. Directed by film veteran Vincent
McEveety, the show dealt with two rodeo cowboys, an old hand and a neo-
phyte, who drank, gambled, stayed broke, and had no luck with women.
Work, the old hand remarked early on, spoils the dignity of cowboys,
especially rodeo cowboys. It was, however, encouraging to hear rodeo
performers refer to themselves as "jocks" and to observe a closer portrait
of rodeo groupies than television had dared to present theretofore.

ities surrounding the National Football League's Super Bowl XII game between Dallas and Denver.[12] Supporters of both teams affected cowboy dress — Denver's fans strained sartorial credibility by insisting upon orange cowboy hats — and ribbed each other with quips about the possible relationships between Cowboys (Dallas) and Broncos (Denver); for example, "Cowboys break broncos," and "Broncos throw cowboys." The violent image of professional football is perhaps heightened by reference to a cowboy connection, but whatever the case, cowboy attire is sported by fans, cheerleaders, and bandsmen of several NFL teams, including such cis-Mississippi stalwarts as the Washington Redskins (who boast thereby a profusion of images) and the Baltimore Colts. To a lesser extent cowboy imagery enlivens professional baseball and professional basketball, especially in the state of Texas (Rangers, Spurs). Still professional teams cannot even begin to approach the amateurs in evoking cowboy imagery, and red cowboy hats may perch atop the heads of college football fans in Alabama as frequently as they adorn pates in Oklahoma or Nebraska, where their presence might be expected.[13] Whether the athletes are amateurs or professionals, however, an afternoon at the game is for the fans an afternoon of escape, a time of vicarious pleasure, and in the environment of the stadium or the arena the image of the cowboy holds reserved seats and a season ticket.

Red cowboy hats are ludicrous, of course — they are kindergarten attire for children who have not yet grasped the playground reality of saner colors like those urged upon their

[12] It was displayed as well on the cover of *Time*, January 16, 1978.

[13] Any examination of cowboy imagery in college football should begin with Gary Shaw, *Meat on the Hoof: The Hidden World of Texas Football* (New York: St. Martin's Press, 1972). It should be understood, of course, that Texas is always an extreme example.

parents by proprietors of western-wear stores — but they do not betoken the utter debasement of cowboy imagery in the adult world. That privilege is reserved to professional wrestling, a charade in the guise of sport, an ethically bankrupt spectacle that, precisely because of its bankruptcy, reveals much about the American mind. Many professional wrestlers evoke the image of the cowboy hero, and by presenting that image amidst the sham of the grunt-and-groan circuit, they give yet another evidence of its primacy.

Professional wrestling matches are miniature dramas wherein each fall represents the curtain between acts and the cast consists of clearly defined heroes and villains in starring roles, supported by well-meaning but (when the chips are down) hopelessly inept referees and a throng of frustrated and occasionally bloodthirsty spectators. Professional wrestling is soap opera in a ring, and its attraction lies in its ability to manipulate the emotions of the audience and to leave that audience (the promoters hope) begging for more. Villains are Germans, Russians, and, lately, Arabs, representing the forces of evil that make life such a hassle on the six o'clock news or at the gas station. Heroes represent the spectators, who do not have the confidence or the ability to beat the hell out of their oppressors but who will pay a few dollars to see someone else do it for them. Professional wrestling provides the catharsis of expiation by proxy. The hero will set things right. Indeed, it is as if the hero could end the energy crisis by felling Akbar the Arab with a flying head scissors.

The sociology of the thing is fascinating, and when one recalls that cowboys participate, it could be viewed as a recapitulation of the B western. But professional wrestling reflects the values of the people who support it, and the variants in cowboy imagery characteristic of the post-World War II era appear in the wrestling arena as well. Which is to say that some cowboys are villains. Take, for example, "Outlaw" Ron

Bass, who wrestled in the Los Angeles area and the Midwest in the late 1970s, a large, bearded individual who entered the ring wearing chaps, a vest, and a cowboy hat. Interlocking horseshoes decorated the seat of his tights. The wrestling hold Bass used to subdue his opponents was known as the "Texas stampede," and, predictably, it involved bulldogging the adversary and slamming him face first into the mat.[14]

Some cowboys in professional wrestling demonstrate the sort of ethical schizophrenia characteristic of the psychological western films of the 1950s. Who knows what they will do in the ring? These fellows are likely to be with you one minute and against you the next. A classic story concerns "Cowboy" Bill Watts, former University of Oklahoma wrestler and, in 1965, the tag-team partner of Bruno Sammartino, a well-known New York-area wrestler and occasional World Wide Wrestling Federation heavyweight champ. Early that year Watts and Sammartino met the Golden Terror and Smasher Sloan in a New Jersey arena, and Watts, in addition to allowing the bad guys to wipe up the mat with his partner (he refused to extend his hand for the tag that would provide surcease of Sammartino's sorrow), helped the enemy cause by kicking his injured buddy. That paved the way, naturally enough, for several lucrative matches between Watts and Sammartino and led to the eventual destruction of Watts's cowboy hat and western jacket at the hands of an enraged Sammartino. Thereafter Watts alternated between roles heroic and villainous — once he joined with fellow Oklahoma alumnus Wahoo McDaniel in a heroic cowboy-and-Indian tag team — until he retired and became a wrestling promoter and partner of wrestling magnate Leroy McGuirk.[15]

---

[14] The hold was hardly original. Years earlier "Cowboy" Bob Ellis had introduced the "Bulldog Headlock," an identical maneuver; and "Cowboy" Bill Watts had employed the "Oklahoma Stampede" in imitation of Ellis.

If the pseudo-sport of professional wrestling represents, in fact, the ultimate debasement of the cowboy image, it nevertheless shares one quality with the bona fide sports noted here: it is taken seriously by its followers. Fans, be they aficionados of professional wrestling, football, rodeo, or whatever, are all of a piece, and an intense, enthusiastic and vocal piece it is too. Johan Huizinga, writing in the 1930s, traced the evolution of the elements of play in human culture to their contemporary manifestation in sports and observed in the process a "tendency to over-seriousness."[16] It is a collective tendency of spectators, certainly, and of many — if not most — athletes (we may exclude professional wrestlers, with apologies to those who take themselves seriously and a sly wink to those who only pretend to). Thus the attendant imagery of sport has more than a casual impact upon the mind of the spectator. On one level sport extends the image of the cowboy hero in an apparently superficial manner, but on another level it personalizes that image for spectator and athlete alike by affording yet another opportunity for direct participation in presenting the image. The rodeo performer accordingly believes that he is a cowboy and possessed of a place in cowboy history, whatever that may be. The professional wrestler, by claiming the cowboy image, evokes responses from fans that are, whatever their effect on the fans themselves, essential to the emotional manipulation that is the wrestler's stock in trade. The football devotee who wears cowboy garb in support of his favorite team is a phenomenon perhaps more complex than these others (or at least there can be no very clear analysis of what goes on in his head), but he is surely

[15] Joe Jares, *Whatever Happened to Gorgeous George?* (Englewood Cliffs, N.J.: Prentice-Hall, 1974), pp. 70-71.

[16] J. Huizinga, *Homo Ludens: A Study of the Play-Element in Culture* (Boston: Beacon Press, 1955), p. 199.

aware of some sort of tradition and his participation in it.[17] The benefit or detriment of these kinds of participation for the individuals who experience them may be determined only individually and within related contexts suggested in the preceding chapters. Athletics, for many people, may be nothing more than a different way to play cowboy — if, in view of the game, the ways of playing are very different after all.

[17] See Michener, *Sports in America*, chap. 2.

.9.
Growing Up –
And Down

ARTHUR MORECAMP SENT the first fictive cowboys up the trail from Texas in 1878. Writing under the pseudonym Thomas Pilgrim, Morecamp produced in that year an opus entitled *The Live Boys; or, Charlie and Nasho in Texas*, which was, the subtitle said, "A narrative relating to two boys, one a Texan, the other a Mexican. Showing their life on the great Texas cattle trail, and their adventures in the Indian Territory, Kansas, and northern Texas; embracing many thrilling adventures."[1] Two years later Pilgrim progressed to a discussion of cowboys doing something else in *Live Boys in the Black Hills; or, The Young Texas Gold Hunters*, principally a tale of miners and Indians.[2] The books were intended for a juvenile audience, but their larger significance involved their early use of the trail drive as a dramatic setting for cowboy fiction. The

---

[1] Thomas Pilgrim (pseud. Arthur Morecamp), *The Live Boys; or, Charlie and Nasho in Texas* (Boston: Lee and Shepard, 1878).

[2] Thomas Pilgrim (pseud. Arthur Morecamp), *Live Boys in the Black Hills; or The Young Texas Gold Hunters,* (Boston: Lee and Shepard, 1880).

possibilities of the trail were not recognized immediately by other writers — Cody and Ingraham had not yet invented the cowboy hero — but at least a precedent had been established. The public would be occupied with the doings of either dime-novel horsemen or the sedentary cowboys of Owen Wister's *The Virginian* (1902) for several decades. Although Andy Adam's *The Log of a Cowboy* — a memoir presented as a novel — appeared in 1903, not until the publication of Emerson Hough's *North of 36* in the summer of 1923 did trail-drive fiction capture the popular imagination.[3] Thereafter the literary descendants of Morecamp's "live boys" would make regular ascents from Texas to trail's end, though rather more for adult readers than for juvenile ones.

Hough's book, like Wister's, was a love story, which made it a book for adults. There was, in the early years of the twentieth century, a good deal of that sort of cowboy fiction, and we have already seen something of the effect of it in Chapter 2. But the point to be made here is that cowboy love stories brought the cowboy hero into the adult consciousness and made him a commodity to be shared by two distinct age groups. Cody's Buck Taylor blazed one trail, to be followed later by B-film and comic-book cowboy heroes, for a predominantly juvenile market; and Wister, Hough, Eugene Manlove Rhodes, and others marked a second, for a readership interested in melodrama. They intersected occasionally, as we shall see, but in time the second trail grew at the expense of the first, until, a century after Morecamp's books appeared, one could say that the cowboy hero existed almost solely in and for the adult world.

The cowboy hero survived melodrama and went on to better literary things. Paperback reprints of *The Virginian* and

---

[3] Emerson Hough, *North of 36* (New York: D. Appleton and Company, 1923).

the seemingly countless novels of Zane Grey have kept melodrama — and love — alive, of course, but these are not the best
evidences of the cowboy hero's place in American fiction.
They remain popular, and that is an important consideration;
but the interesting thing is that the cowboy has been able to
stimulate serious writers as well as frivolous ones, so that his
image rests upon the substantial cultural underpinning of literature and is thus an image of transcendent appeal. There is
no need to segregate the serious from the popular, in fiction
or in anything else, because culture has an unassailable unity;
but one may at least distinguish between levels of culture to
demonstrate the relationships between them and the ways
in which they amplify and alter images for their respective
audiences.[4] For example, the trail theme introduced by Morecamp and popularized by Hough found expression in some
of the best and some of the worst cowboy fiction, and that
situation suggests a great deal of imagerial alteration and
amplification.

Zane Grey published *The Trail Driver* in 1936.[5] As a novel
it owed much to Hough's *North of 36*. It was, at bottom, a love
story, and the trail drive provided a setting wherein the cowboy hero might resolve his personal conflicts and thereby
render himself suitable for the holy estate of matrimony.
Like Hough, Grey recognized something of the epic quality
of the long drive, but, also like Hough, he was unable to do
much about it. Grey's cowboys are a bit saltier than Hough's,
but not salty enough to neutralize the saccharine in the plot.
Those who survive the mandatory gunplay at trail's end must
cease their cowboying anyway, since their girlfriends will not
tolerate it. Such melodramatic conventions seldom improve

[4] See Don D. Walker, "Notes Toward a Literary Criticism of the
Western," *Journal of Popular Culture* 7 (Winter, 1973): 728-41.
[5] Zane Grey, *The Trail Driver*, (New York: Harper & Row, 1936).

with age, but they could still be found in cowboy fiction fifty years after Hough established them.[6]

The cowboys in these syrupy novels were at the end of the trail and, more often than not, the ends of their occupational ropes as well. More sophisticated writers understood that the long drive was not a protracted trip to the altar and that larger questions might be considered. For them fiction was a meditation upon history, and the trail theme acquired a significance only hinted at by Hough and Grey. The trail became a symbol for initiation, representing the socializing process by which boys pass into manhood. The trail was preparation for something else; it was a beginning, not an end. Jack Schaefer, in *Monte Walsh* (1963), described a half-dozen drives in not many more pages to chart the physical and psychological growth of his protagonist.[7] In *The Bright Feathers* (1965), John Culp's teenage cowboys learned their lessons on the way home (suggesting, thereby, that two years on the trail left lessons to be learned).[8] But the classic use of the trail-as-initiation theme was surely William Dale Jennings's, in *The Cowboys* (1971), the novel that was the basis for Mark Rydell's film. Here the cowboys were truly boys, taken into service by a cattleman because no older hands were available. In fact, they were recruited at the local schoolhouse. With the cattleman and his cook as their mentors, they learned about more than cattle; and later, after they had avenged their employer's death by murdering his murderers, and when they were

[6] See, for example, Mel Marshall, *Longhorns North* (New York: Ballantine Books, 1969); and Cliff Farrell, *Patchsaddle Drive* (Garden City, N.Y.: Doubleday & Company, 1972).

[7] Jack Schaefer, *Monte Walsh* (Boston: Houghton Mifflin Company, 1963).

[8] John Culp, *The Bright Feathers* (New York: Holt, Rinehart and Winston, 1965).

confused by the new responsibilities of manhood, even to the point of regretting their justifiable homicides, the cook told them not to worry. "All that happened," he said, "was we all got ourselfs swept up in life."[9]

There is a certain mystique about the long drive considered as initiation or (at the very least) as educational experience. In any strict historical sense the trail, unless it was prelude to returning home, could only represent initiation into a comparatively small and statistically abnormal society — comparable perhaps to classical homosexual warrior societies or even the Caribbean *boucaniers* of an earlier day — but within the context of literature it may be the best American symbol of the process of growing up. Huck Finn, we may recall, went neither to war nor to college to complete the maturation begun by his escape with Jim and his recognition of the nature of slavery; rather, he lit out for Indian Territory, the archetypal American kid who grew up by westering (though not in the way we might think, according to John Seelye).[10] The problem, of course, is that Huck sought to escape civilization (whose name was Aunt Sally), and so, by and large, does the cowboy hero. The image of the cowboy hero as a rugged individualist, an outsider, does not square with whatever societal demands there may be for initiation — indeed, the cowboy has fled from those demands and their suggestion of responsibility — but, again, his is a restricted society. Moreover, if the cowboy as a cultural artifact may be taken as a symbol of what Americans wish they might become, then the trail can be viewed as his choice of experiences, a personal selection for his rite of passage, a symbol of the option that Americans believe they possess. In that sense the cowboy on the trail is everyman growing up.

[9] Jennings, *The Cowboys*, p. 219.
[10] See John Seelye, *The Kid* (New York: Viking Press, 1972), a literary prank about which it is better not to say too much.

And the process, once begun, never really ends. Some people, however, postpone the beginning for one reason or another, and at some point the ritual of initiation becomes only a demonstration of naïveté, as it is for the characters in Robert Flynn's *North to Yesterday* (1967) and, to a lesser extent, Robert Day's *The Last Cattle Drive* (1977).[11] But here the image of heroism derives from whatever nobility one finds in pointless struggles against hopeless odds. Closer to the mark is the experience of Levi Dougherty in Clair Huffaker's *The Cowboy and the Cossack* (1973)[12] or of Rowdy Yates, who grew in wisdom, if not in stature, once each week on the endless trails of "Rawhide."

Fictive cowboys also lived on ranches, and seventy years after Owen Wister wrote, they were often still the literary kin of the famed Virginian. One might grow up on a ranch, surely; and the combination of aging and that sedentary life led to a greater acceptance of social responsibility than did life on the trail. Schaefer's Monte Walsh settled down, avoided marriage, survived the marriage of his best friend, grew old, and died trying to save the lives of others. In William Decker's *To Be a Man* (1967), Roscoe Banks, an aged cowboy, died trying to defend the small community that had adopted him when his days as a ranch hand were over.[13] Homer Bannon, of Larry McMurtry's *Horseman, Pass By* (1961), survived wilder days to become the patriarch of a questionable clan and to break only when his ranch — his dream — broke, the

[11] Robert Flynn, *North to Yesterday* (New York: Alfred A. Knopf, 1967); Robert Day, *The Last Cattle Drive*, (New York: G. P. Putnam's Sons, 1977).

[12] Clair Huffaker, *The Cowboy and the Cossack*, (New York: Trident Press, 1973).

[13] William Decker, *To Be a Man* (Boston: Little, Brown and Company, 1967).

economic victim of disease and steadfast veterinarians armed with rifles.[14]

These are adult images of the cowboy, and it is hardly surprising that they exist largely in the medium of print. Curious things happen, however, when they are translated into other media. Film, for example, did little to enhance the character of Monte Walsh or Homer Bannon, yet it provided the vehicle for the presentation of Will Penny — Tom Gries's production bore that name in 1968 — a cowboy without literary antecedents but one nevertheless deftly limned. Penny was another cowboy concocted for adults, but he is in the history of film probably only another B-film hero, stripped of the gloss of convention. Will Penny was true to his calling and true to his code and thus could overcome his status in the world as illiterate booby; and he was good with a gun. Like Monte Walsh, Penny had outlived his biological usefulness — or at least his desire to be biologically (and therefore socially) useful — and in his adherence to the tenets of cowboydom he was the arrested adolescent, perhaps better described as the adult "growing down."

That is one aspect of it — the juvenilization of the cowboy for adults — but the cowboy hero was from time to time made to "grow down" for children as well, and occasionally the process resulted in radical changes in certain cowboy characters. The case of Hopalong Cassidy is instructive on the subject of the behavioral relationships between words and pictures.

Clarence E. Mulford invented Hopalong Cassidy for a series of short stories collected first in book form in 1907, when Mulford was twenty-four. The original Cassidy was a crusty individual, a working cowboy who demonstrated prodigious capacities for consuming alcohol and tobacco, spouting trivial

<hr />

[14] Larry McMurtry, *Horseman, Pass By* (New York: Harper & Row, 1961).

vulgarity, and cheating at cards. He hopped along because of an old bullet wound (his name used to be Bill Cassidy), and that perhaps added something to whatever natural irritability he derived from being a redhead. At any rate, he was a two-gun gunslinger with homicidal tendencies.

Mulford's Cassidy became a western staple in the 1920s and developed a curious literary history. His creator was an easterner who first saw the West seventeen years after writing his initial western story and who fortified his fiction with information gleaned from a massive private library of western Americana, all indexed and cross-indexed on thousands of file cards. The Cassidy stories, therefore, were at least based upon a perception of reality, even though Mulford did not linger long in contemplation of the actual locales or the sorts of people about which he wrote. Mulford was a contemporary of Zane Grey's, but he eschewed Grey's penchant for romantic tales, believing them to be distortions of the western experience — and this despite the obvious success of Grey's books. Nevertheless, the uncouth Cassidy did marry in 1910; but Mulford played fast and loose with connubial bliss, publishing stories out of sequence when it suited him, until, in 1924, he killed off Mrs. Cassidy and his hero's child. Mulford preferred to write about men anyway, and Cassidy was certainly that. So were his plenteous sidekicks, who, with names like Tex Ewalt, Red Connors, and Mesquite Jenkins, added much to Mulford's hairy-chested fiction.[15]

Moviemaker Harry Sherman saw great potential in the Cassidy character, and in 1935 he approached Mulford with plans for a series of films about Hopalong. The first of sixty-six Cassidy movies appeared later that year, all starring

[15] Tuska, *The Filming of the West*, pp. 312-15.

William Boyd, a screen presence as different from Mulford's creation as one could possibly imagine. The difference was not intentional, however, for Sherman had tried to capture the flavor of the original Cassidy by offering the role to James Gleason, a forty-nine-year-old character actor of slight stature and mean visage. But Gleason wanted too much money, so Sherman next asked David Niven, a twenty-six-year-old extra who declined the job in anticipation of better things. William Boyd was the third choice, and he became Hopalong Cassidy.

Or rather Hopalong Cassidy became William Boyd. Mulford's Cassidy died in 1935, when Boyd rode across the screen as a blond, black-clad superhero to bring the world a "Hoppy" who neither drank nor smoked, never swore, seldom dallied with the ladies, cheated at nothing, and always triumphed because he was a paragon of virtue with a lightning draw. These were the years of the Depression, when escapism was the order of the day in entertainment and when the cowboy hero enjoyed a new popularity — and the Boyd films were popular.[16] A decade later they were less so, perhaps because World War II had brought fresher (and sometimes real) heroes. Boyd thoroughly identified — and was thoroughly identified by the public — with the Cassidy character and, type-cast as that cowboy hero, he could find no other work in motion pictures. Boyd bought the rights to his Cassidy films after Sherman decided to make no more, and eventually he sold them to television, where, in abbreviated form, they first appeared in 1948.

Television brought Hopalong Cassidy to more children than Harry Sherman could have imagined, and Boyd became a star all over again. Within two years Boyd's television success led

---

[16] See Andrew Bergman, *We're in the Money: Depression America and Its Films* (New York: New York University Press, 1971), chap. 7.

to a radio series — starring Boyd — and a syndicated comic strip. Entrepreneurs marketed tons of "Hoppy" merchandise. Cassidy cowboy costumes were especially popular with youngsters, and in the early 1950s manufacturers reported a nationwide shortage of black dye as a result of producing so many items of Hopalong-like attire.[17] In 1951, Boyd began making half-hour films specifically for television. He eventually completed fifty-two of them, and in the mid-1970s they were still available in syndication.

So Mulford's rangeland tough became William Boyd's personification of goodness in the saddle. Hopalong Cassidy was no longer a cowboy, thanks to Boyd's emendations; rather, he was a fantasy for children — a sheriff, a detective, a righteous gunfighter, or whatever the occasion called for in the way of a paladin-cum-factotum. The role changed Boyd's life as much as Boyd's portrayals changed Cassidy's image. In the 1920s, Boyd had acquired a penchant for drinking and gambling that even Hopalong himself would have admired. He divorced two wives in that decade, and he would divorce again and remarry in the mid-1930s. But the experience of being Hoppy put an end to such doings, and Boyd's life became exemplary. He was, after all, a children's hero. "When you've got parents saying what a wonderful guy Hoppy is, what the hell do you do?" he once mused. "You've got to be a wonderful guy."[18]

Rumor has it that when Clarence E. Mulford first went to the theater to see what Sherman had done with his character, he passed out from shock. Smelling salts revived him then, and the money he made from the cinematic version of his work

---

[17] Dunning, *Tune in Yesterday,* p. 290; Oliver Jensen, "Hopalong Hits the Jackpot," *Life,* June 12, 1950, pp. 63-70.

[18] Quoted in Boyd's obituary notice in *Newsweek,* September 25, 1972, p. 71. See also David Zinman, *Saturday Afternoon at the Bijou* (New York: Arlington House, 1973), pp. 154-55.

sustained him later. The movies continued Cassidy's peculiar literary odyssey, for they prompted the reappearance of the Mulford books. But, strangely, the new editions were rewritten. Again the old Hopalong bit the dust, his bad habits expunged from print by the screen image of William Boyd.[19] The books were fitter for children that way, and besides, Boyd *was* Hopalong Cassidy. He had grown down to it, as much lost in the fantasy of his own making as were the kids who cheered his victories.

The image of the cowboy hero is now seldom presented to juvenile audiences, to judge by his current absence from comic books and Saturday-morning television. The old heroes, like Autry and Rogers, who followed Hoppy's hoofbeats into the video wasteland, contributed substantially to the juvenilization of the cowboy in the early 1950s, but by the end of the decade they had succumbed to the riders of the Ponderosa and Gil Favor's trail crew. When children went on to caped crusaders and men of steel, the cowboy remained with the grownups, and literary traditions were fulfilled. In the context of adult entertainment, the cowboy might appear as lover or fighter, old man or youngster, loner or community member; but he was in the process of becoming — and that has to do with age and the experience brought by time.

There is the example of Joe Buck, from James Leo Herlihy's *Midnight Cowboy,* filmed by John Schlesinger in 1969.[20] He is the country-come-to-town (and very nearly to no good end) cowboy who equates manhood less with relationships or responsibilities than with the gift of his loins, and he attempts to conquer the city as he would some innocent daughter in

---

[19] Horwitz, *They Went Thataway,* p. 123.

[20] James Leo Herlihy, *Midnight Cowboy* (New York: Simon and Schuster, 1965).

the back seat back home. But he is the innocent, and so he barely survives. His innocence is tarnished, and he must at last endure the death of his only friend on the threshold of the dream they both pursue, though his own continued survival is in serious doubt. He is a cowboy growing up.

There is the example of Little Joe and his brothers Hoss and Adam, all sons of Ben Cartwright and heirs to the Ponderosa on television's "Bonanza." There life is suspended in the freeze frame of familial consistency for fourteen years, during which time only Adam dares leave home. Hoss and Little Joe stay, one to die and the other to marry — devastating events that brought network cancellation. In syndication still, they are cowboys not permitted to grow up.

These examples suggest a false dichotomy. They reflect not different views of life or even different levels of culture but the same response to circumstance. Joe Buck, with neither family nor friends, must grow up to find both comfort and security. The sons of Ben Cartwright need not, for they have those things in abundance. Necessity, these examples suggest, breeds either change or nostalgia, depending on the nature of the need. The individual contemplating the cowboy protagonist contemplates only himself and finds therein both explanation of and justification for the epic journeys of all people from the cradle to the grave — the long drive to trail's end.

That is no mere maudlin metaphor, inasmuch as by our fictions we define ourselves. Indeed, we often are our fictions. William Boyd was his, certainly, and so were Hart and Mix and many others. But so were their audiences; and if each human being has a mythic life superimposed upon the real one,[21] then literature and film do offer valid metaphor, for life

---

[21] See Joe McGinniss, *Heroes* (New York: Viking Press, 1976), which deals with politicians, not cowboys.

and art are of a piece. Tim McCoy recalled working cowboys who regularly spent their money at movie houses or read Grey and Wister and Mulford to sustain their visions of themselves and to comprehend their place in time. That is why anyone reads or watches. It has to do with growing, with becoming, and it is another reason why the cowboy hero exists.[22]

[22] Tim McCoy (with Ronald McCoy), *Tim McCoy Remembers the West: An Autobiography* (Garden City, N.Y.: Doubleday & Company, 1977), pp. 232-33. Consider also William D. Wittliff and Sara Clark, *Thaddeus Rose and Eddie* (Los Angeles: Pinnacle Books, 1978), a novel based on Wittliff's screenplay for a critically acclaimed CBS television movie about two middle-aged cowboys learning to grow up.

·10·
A Bore
at Last

THE PRECEDING CHAPTERS suggest that the cowboy hero serves two principal functions in American culture: he transmits social values, and he sells merchandise. The first of these is a political (in the sense of educational or, more often, indoctrinational) function, and the second is an economic one. They are interrelated to the extent that the first guarantees the efficacy of the second, while the second exploits and thereby extends the imagery of the first.[1] The functions may appear to be contradictory, but in fact they are not, for within the context of what is known as "the American way" they are merely opposite sides of the same coin. Truth, honor, justice, pre-

---

[1] They are cyclical as well. Thus the cowboy hero may disappear momentarily in entertainment, where his political function is performed, but remain in advertising to continue his economic function. The advertising preserves the imagery until the hero returns to entertain and so educate. Instructive is Jeffrey Schrank, *Snap, Crackle, and Popular Taste: The Illusion of Free Choice in America* (New York: Dell Publishing Co., 1977), especially chaps. 4, 7. See also Daniel J. Boorstin, *Democracy and Its Discontents: Reflections on Everyday America* (New York: Random House, 1974), pp. 38-42.

paredness, righteousness, free enterprise, and a great many more noble nouns are of a piece in the commonly accepted system of beliefs that Americans think separates them from other people, and the cowboy hero stands squarely in the middle of it all. Not by accident is the cowboy most commonly announced as the *American* cowboy, even though the adjective raises the obvious question, What other kind of cowboy is there?[2]

Popular history describes the cowboy as "a truly unique American type."[3] Popular entertainment has often gone farther than that. On Sunday afternoon, January 7, 1940, when "Gene Autry's Melody Ranch" program premiered on CBS radio, announcer Ken Ellington's tautological script made much of the Americanism of the new venture. The cowboy, according to the script, was an "American symbol," and, as a cowboy, Autry himself was a "symbol of the clean thinking, honesty, and integrity of the American people." Autry's guitar and his music are "as American, as natural, as typical of this nation of ours as, well, say, apple pie or corn pone." Indeed, Autry had become a success because he contributed something "new" to America. His was "purely American entertainment." And so forth.[4] If H. L. Mencken had listened, he might have been moved to express a new prejudice, even though one

[2] However close he may have been occupationally, the gaucho was no cowboy, despite Stephen Paullada, *Rawhide and Song* (New York: Vantage Press, 1963). A better study is Madaline Wallis Nichols, *The Gaucho* (Durham, N.C.: Duke University Press, 1942), which describes the strong political function of the gaucho image in Argentine culture.

[3] "Editorial," *Wild West,* June, 1969, p. 4.

[4] This initial program, which told the story of Autry's discovery by Will Rogers in an Oklahoma railroad station, simply reeked of such rhetoric. The script emphasized fantasy and escapism as healthy pastimes for Americans tired of the political and economic problems of the day, and it promised to take listeners "as far away from the outside world as possible."

of his dating from the 1920s would have characterized adequately the social context of all that imagery. "The *boobus Americanus,*" he had written,

is a bird that knows no closed season — and if he won't come down to Texas oil stock, or one-night cancer cures, or building lots in Swampshurst, he will always come down to Inspiration and Optimism, whether political, theological, pedagogical, literary, or economic.[5]

In this case the decoy was inspiration in the guise of the cowboy hero, a character who ignored — and through whom one might also ignore — the Depression, Europe, and the other unsavory details of 1940. The program pitched Autry to the people and Wrigley's Doublemint to merchants, who were told that they might help promote Autry's brand of Americanism by stocking the sponsor's brand of gum. Here the political and economic functions of the cowboy hero were conjoined and showcased: Autry became the country boy who made good in the movies (a real Horatio Alger story, said the script) by being typically American, and the merchant received praise as one selected to avail himself of the economic bootstraps offered by the good people at Wrigley's.[6]

The cowboy hero is, as we have seen elsewhere, a symbol of individualism, which quality Theodore Roosevelt, Frederick Jackson Turner, and others had given currency in the late nineteenth century as one of the essentials of the American way. Autry's Alger image was in keeping with the tenets of individualism, inasmuch as "self-help" philosophies were

---

[5] James T. Farrell, ed., *H. L. Mencken: Prejudices, A Selection* (New York: Vintage Books, n.d.) p. 94.

[6] The prevalence of such simplemindedness is discussed in Bruce E. Coad, "The Alger Hero," in *Heroes of Popular Culture,* ed. Ray B. Browne, Marshall Fishwick, and Michael T. Marsden (Bowling Green, Ohio: Bowling Green University Popular Press, 1972), pp. 42-51.

deemed to be of central importance, having the endorsement of thinkers ranging in kind and quality from Benjamin Franklin to Elbert Hubbard.[7] Yet Americanism is suggestive more of shared than of individual behavior, and in that regard the cowboy hero, if he is to be typically American, loses something. The point, of course, is that his political and economic functions are necessarily collective. The cowboy hero transmits social values and obviously could not exist without society; the structure of his image requires both a stage upon which to play and an audience for which to perform. The cowboy hero sells merchandise and could not succeed without a marketplace; and individualism and economics are mutually exclusive terms in all but the murkiest doctrinal mélanges.

If the cowboy hero is an integral part of the American national mythology (and here I mean mythology broadly conceived and including both politics and economics), he is also an item useful for the perpetuation and projection of that mythology. The cowboy hero has a certain political utility as an item of cultural export. Dean MacCannell has cited as "our official version of our contributions to international culture" a poster distributed by the United States Travel Service for European consumption.[8] The poster displays, in various typefaces, nineteen words or phrases selected to evoke images of America, images that presumably would attract the potential foreign visitor. Of the nineteen words or phrases seventeen are proper nouns, and of those, sixteen name places or things. Only one names an animate object: "cowboy." Among the places and things are "ranch" and "rodeo," "Grand Canyon" and "bar-b-que." Thus 26 per cent of the images are western,

[7] Conal Furay, *The Grass-Roots Mind in America: The American Sense of Absolutes* (New York: New Viewpoints, 1977), p. 35.

[8] Dean MacCannell, *The Tourist: A New Theory of the Leisure Class* (New York: Schocken Books, 1976), p. 182.

and nearly 16 per cent are specifically related to the cowboy and his occupations.[9]

Such emphasis is not misplaced, given the fairly widespread preoccupation in western Europe with the history and culture of western America. The cowboy image accompanies country-and-western music in Great Britain, and the Associated Press occasionally reports on the thousands of Britons who purchase jeans, Stetsons, boots, and even gunbelts to wear to country-music festivals in London or to clubs featuring that variety of American entertainment. The Westerners, an organization of western-history buffs founded in Chicago in 1944, boasts chapters in London, Paris, Gothenburg, Munich, and other European cities — whose members may wear cowboy clothes because of the "unrealized longing of those left behind" for a chance to participate in the making of this nation of immigrants.[10] The interest in things western is hardly new, having a strong foundation in nineteenth-century European popular fiction, notably the dozens of blood-and-thunder novels of Germany's Karl May, creator of Old Shatterhand and his Apache sidekick, Winnetou.[11] May died in 1912, but hundreds of thousands of copies of his novels are still sold annually, and they have been translated into twenty languages. How-

[9] The other words and phrases are "Supermarket," "Niagara Falls," "Weekend," "A-OK," "Drugstore," "Hot Dog," "Musicals," "Jeep," "Snack Bar," "Jazz," "Cola," "Pop," "On the Rocks," and "Chewing Gum." Interestingly, the Indian, a significant attraction for the western tourist trade, is completely ignored.

[10] The words are Gertrud Hafner's, quoted in *Buckskin Bulletin*, Spring-Summer, 1972, p. 2

[11] See Richard H. Cracroft, "The American West of Karl May," *American Quarterly* 19 (Summer, 1967): 249-58; D. L. Ashliman, "The Novel of Western Adventure in Nineteenth-Century Germany," *Western American Literature* 8 (Summer, 1968): 133-45; and Ray Allen Billington, "The Wild West in Norway, 1877," *Western Historical Quarterly* 7 (July, 1976): 271-78.

ever distorted May's portrait of the West may have been (his Apaches went about in canoes), its images were as persuasive as the peculiar visions of European film directors like Sergio Leone, whose work played well to American audiences and popularized "spaghetti westerns" after it had proved successful in Italy.[12]

Still these were European images of the West, as Gothic in their design as thirteenth-century architecture. The novels of May and others led to a plethora of western comic strips in the Continental nations beginning in the 1920s and then to the cinema. As derivative and imitative as the images were, they were also different, even bizarre, and they persist yet. Europeans, Maurice Horn has noted, "look upon the Western as a modern allegory of the eternal struggle between good and evil, and see in the lone cowboy the rightful heir of the wandering knight of medieval epics and novels of chivalry."[13] That would certainly make a difference. If Horn is correct, however, then European audiences have no more accurate a perception of history than American audiences do.

These images have little connection with Americanism considered as a system of values, but the cowboy hero as an item of export often travels abroad in company with some of the principal artifacts of American culture. The most important of these are television programs, series long defunct on American networks but available to foreign broadcasters at nominal rates. In many of the world's technological backwaters such ancient fare is prime-time programming. Andrew R. Horowitz

[12] See Richard T. Jameson, "Something to Do with Death: A Fistful of Sergio Leone," *Film Comment*, March-April, 1973, pp. 8-16; Laurence Staig and Tony Williams, *Italian Western: The Opera of Violence* (London: Lorimer Press, 1975); and Fenin and Everson, *The Western*, chap. 19.

[13] Maurice Horn, *Comics of the American West* (New York: Winchester Press, 1977), p. 174.

estimated in 1975 that in a given week approximately 400 million people in ninety nations would witness the doings of the cowboys on the Ponderosa. In 1974 prime-time television in Nigeria featured, in addition to "Bonanza," two other cowboy-oriented shows, "Bronco" and "The Big Valley," all at the expense of local programming, which costs more than the American imports. "The impact in Nigeria, as elsewhere," according to Horowitz, "has been to wipe out the economic base for local program production."[14] Presumably more American retreads will fill the void, and the cowboy hero and the values he espouses will survive in Lagos, even when he is in temporary eclipse in Peoria.

And eclipse in Peoria — or anywhere else — is not a bad thing for the cowboy hero, even though whenever it happens there are more than enough critics prepared to state without reservation that the situation is permanent. We are told periodically that there will be no more cowboys, for, if the hero's demise is not yet an accomplished fact, it is certainly imminent. Among journalists nowadays "last cowboys" are in vogue, and the label is freely attached to everyone from truck drivers to John Wayne and occasionally even to working cowboys, to whom it may best apply.[15] Hardheaded cultural conservatives say that this is nonsense and that the cowboy hero will survive because the "western story is indestructible — in no danger of being replaced."[16] It seems so, for the reason

[14] Andrew R. Horowitz, "The Global Bonanza of American TV," in *Media Culture: Television, Radio, Records, Books, Magazines, Newspapers, Movies*, ed. James Monaco (New York: Dell Publishing Co., 1978), p. 118.

[15] In addition to James Bacon, "John Wayne, the Last Cowboy," *Us*, June 27, 1978, pp. 23-25, see also Stern, *Trucker*, and Kramer, *The Last Cowboy.*

[16] C. L. Sonnichsen, "The West That Wasn't," *American West* 14 (November-December, 1977): p. 13.

that America has too few heroes to risk discarding any: but to leave it at that is to beg several questions.

The consistency of heroes and the popular need for them is one thing, but the hero's mode of conveyance in culture is quite another. Since World War II the frequency of the hero's appearance in electronic media has been the measure of his popularity, and the easy assumption is that if he is not around then we have done with him, finally and completely.[17] But, like libraries or computers, the electronic media never really forget anything, and the hero is still there, stored safely on film, tape, or vinyl, but most of all as an idea, only waiting to be revived. Because he has to do with merchandise — indeed, because at the level of popular entertainment he is himself merchandise — his mass appeal is subject to cyclical influences affecting the audiovisual marketplace. The hero may be lost temporarily to one medium, only to reappear in another one; but given the unity of culture, he is never lost entirely. Changes in his image are not at issue in this process, but they may be affected by it.

The content of no single medium is an accurate measure of popularity, of course, and popularity has little to do with cultural validity. Still, if networks present no cowboy programs, then independent stations do, and there are local late movies on nearly every television channel, wherein heroes might ply their trade. And if the cowboy hero occasionally receives short shrift at the boxoffice, drugstores and supermarkets continue to peddle his paperback adventures. He is available to those who want him, and many do. His cinematic eclipse in the late 1970s is no more ominous with regard to his place in American culture than it was in the early 1930s. The demise of the B-film cowboy in the 1950s heralded nothing but the advent of the television cowboy in the 1950s. And so forth.

[17] See "The New Wilderness," *Time*, December 8, 1975, p. 20.

What the momentary eclipse does is allow the air to clear. Most of what is written about the cowboy hero is produced in periods of national "cowboy mania," times in which his image is widely disseminated and our infatuation with him abundantly clear. The culture climate described by Frantz and Choate in 1955 in their study of the cowboy no longer exists.[18] They wrote in response to a set of circumstances that no longer obtains, and they wrote, much as Andy Adams did, to set the record straight by separating "myth" from "reality." Their point, that media portrayals of cowboys gilded history, was hardly debatable then, and certainly it is not now; but the cowboy hero possesses a bit more cultural, sociological, and economic significance — and a good deal less historical significance — than they were prepared to allow. Their book is but one example, and it is hardly the worst, of the critical scholarship produced in the cowboy heyday of the 1950s. When we recall that the decade was one in which film and fiction, radio and television, and comic strips and comic books were all dealing heavily in cowboy imagery — they coalesced on the subject for the first and last time in the 1950s — then perhaps we can begin to understand how that imagery overwhelmed the spectator and led surely to the conclusion that here was something to be dealt with, and quickly.

"Every hero," Emerson observed, "becomes a bore at last." In the 1950s, the cowboy hero received some unwarranted and altogether hasty assistance in that department from critics who either already thought he was boring, or who sought to make him that way. Their efforts often took peculiar directions. David B. Davis, for example, described the cowboy hero as "the hero of the pre-adolescent, either chronologically or mentally," but then he concluded that, in view of the other available choices for heroes (Nazis, gangsters, Batman), "we

18 Frantz and Choate, *The American Cowboy*, chap. 1.

can be thankful for our silly cowboy."[19] Psychologist Kenneth J. Munden, of the Menninger Foundation, examined the "cowboy myth" and found that it had something to do with the fear of a "weak, powerless, possessed and sexually-dominated mother without a penis."[20] That might have been enough for anybody, but those who wanted more could read the views of Swedish chemist Harry Schein, who saw *High Noon* as a cowboy movie and proclaimed it to be "the most convincing and, likewise, certainly the most honest explanation of American foreign policy."[21] Commentaries like these demonstrated, first, that the cowboy hero was a suitable topic for scholarly journals and, second, that it was possible to say too much about him. Mercifully, the 1950s ended, popular interest subsided, scholarly interest waned, and the air cleared.

The 1960s brought McLuhan and discussions of media and the growth of popular culture as a bona fide academic discipline. The cowboy hero was not the only artifact examined in these contexts, and scholars lavished attention upon myriad other items in the American cultural inventory. What little McLuhan said about cowboys suggested volumes and provided a keystone for the work of several others.[22] The study

---

[19] Davis, "Ten-Gallon Hero," pp. 119, 125.

[20] Kenneth J. Munden, "A Contribution to the Psychological Understanding of the Origin of the Cowboy and His Myth," *American Imago* 15 (Summer, 1958): 146.

[21] Harry Schein, "The Olympian Cowboy," *American Scholar* 24 (Summer, 1955): 316. Schein's analysis of *High Noon* (Gary Cooper is America; the town is the United Nations; the bad guys are Russia, China, and North Korea; and Grace Kelly represents pacifists everywhere) is now embalmed in some American history texts, and solemnly, too. For John Wayne's view of the film, see Zolotow, *Shooting Star,* pp. 257-58.

[22] See Marshall McLuhan and Quentin Fiore, *The Medium Is the Massage* (New York: Bantam Books, 1967), pp. 74-75: and Marshall Fishwick, *The Hero, American Style* (New York: David McKay Company, 1969), p. 69 and, for something of McLuhan-era method, chap. 15.

of popular culture, meanwhile, was largely the work of professors of literature, and the principles of literary criticism applied to the cowboy hero had by the 1970s resulted in scholarly concoctions as strange as any made in the 1950s.[23] The problem here was that popular culture existed as a discipline without a methodology. While McLuhan's followers at least had his theoretical work to guide them, no clear school of theory or method emerged to shape the direction of studies in popular culture, and exponents of popular culture could not even agree on a definition of their field.[24] Yet most of their work made more sense than the investigations of Will Wright, a sociologist whose theory and method led him to conclude that the values of western films are merely reflections of economic philosophies prevalent in America at the time the films were made — a conclusion that considerably befogs our view of the cowboy hero.[25]

The scholarship of the 1960s and 1970s diffused quickly, like chimney smoke on a windy day, because the cowboy hero experienced another eclipse in the mid-1970s. His dissection was then less urgent because, in eclipse, he was less relevant. The effect of his cyclical popularity and its stimulus to scholar-

[23] See, for example, Michael T. Marsden, "Savior in the Saddle: The Sagebrush Testament," in *Focus on the Western*, ed. Nachbar, pp. 93-100, which advances the notion that the "coming of the Western hero is a kind of Second Coming of Christ" (p. 95).

[24] The problem is illustrated by the section entitled "Theories and Methodologies in Popular Culture," in *Journal of Popular Culture* 9 (Fall, 1975): 353-508, which contains twenty-one widely differing perspectives.

[25] Will Wright, *Six Guns and Society: A Structural Study of the Western* (Berkeley: University of California Press, 1975). Wright makes extravagant claims for his work, but his evidence is scant, and his methodology is questionable, and besides that, his title is misleading. The book is useful because it suggests a different direction for film analysis, but that is no justification for its existence in its present form.

ship has been to provide for future investigators a wealth of conceptual frameworks and, more important, the time for contemplation and reassessment of the cowboy hero against new backgrounds. Without that the cowboy hero would indeed become as boring as Emerson's great men. By the time of his most recent evanescence the cowboy hero had been linked to Vietnam through the person of John Wayne; but the 1940s Americanism advocated by Wayne found something less than unanimous approval during the Nixon years. The nearly simultaneous departure of the cowboy hero and the conclusion of American involvement in Vietnam put an end to that, leaving time for more careful assessment of the results of the liaison.[26]

Regardless of the vagaries of scholarship or the media, publications by and for nostalgia buffs reveal feverish obsessions with the cowboy hero, supplying a small but staunch "cowboy underground" with streams of purple prose about their favorite B-film stars. Obituaries are favorite exercises. When Tex Ritter, "America's Most Beloved Cowboy," died in 1974, the underground wallowed in self-pity. Wrote one fan,

Gone he may be. But he has left behind a wealth of memories, all of them happy ones. Gone, did I say? No, not really. So much of him is with us still, and it will always be here to remind us of golden days. In hearts of many millions Tex Ritter dwelt, and there he will always remain.[27]

Death is not a prerequisite for eulogy in the underground. Retirement is sufficient. All one need do is leave memories in

---

[26] Among the results is John Wayne's 1973 record album *America: Why I Love Her* (RCA LSP-4828), which joins patriotic themes with cowboy imagery, both in the liner photographs and in such selections as "Mis Raices Están Aquí."

[27] John Wright, "Tex Ritter," *Remember When*, no. 16 (1974): 6.

which the underground might traffic. So Gene Autry may have been

unaware of the most important thing he was fashioning . . . as one of Hollywood's . . . favorites: Memories. *Memories* fond and warm — of days when life was far less complicated, when Saturday was the greatest day of the week.[28]

The cowboy underground and the cowboy establishment serve similar purposes. The underground preserves and exalts the image of the B-film cowboy, and the establishment perpetuates and praises an (not *the*) image of the historical cowboy. Both safeguard relevant artifacts, and that is their major contribution to American culture. Less useful is their insistence upon mystical interpretations of cowboy imagery.

And here is a further illustration of the benefits of the cyclical popularity of the cowboy hero. The establishment and the underground are relatively small groups, and they hold the image of the cowboy ever before them. Should their views obtain in the larger society, then the image would be ever before us, too, serving as a fetish for some vast cowboy cult or bringing the cowboy to the rim of religious significance. That sort of thing diminishes the vitality of any culture by severing its heroes from its people and enshrining them elsewhere. The Greeks instructed the world on the proper places of gods and heroes in the scheme of things and made it clear that the two entities were not the same. If that is illusion, it is one from which we ought not to be disabused. The cyclical nature of the cowboy hero's popularity in mass media prevents cultural catastrophe. And it keeps his image fresh for the next use.

We have examined several images of the cowboy hero in

[28] James Coral, "Public Cowboy No. 1: Gene Autry," *Remember When*, no. 15 (1974): 5.

this book, and there are more than we might yet consider. Perhaps the most difficult images for many to reconcile with the cowboy hero's status as cultural artifact are his commercial ones. But commercialism is a part of culture; and while critics like George Bluestone might claim that "the compromising pressures of a commercial industry" prevent the cowboy "from becoming truly first-rate,"[29] they have not kept him from inspiring the sort of high culture that even the most finicky patron of the arts would acknowledge. Aaron Copland's ballet suites, *Billy the Kid* and *Rodeo*; Morton Gould's symphony *Cowboy Rhapsody*; Allan Albert's play *Corral*; passages of Roy Harris's *Folk-Song Symphony* — these creations and more bear witness to the benign influence of cowboy imagery. And if they elevate the human spirit, as art will do, are they then so very different from the novels of Grey or the films of Mix, which, though they speak to other levels of experience, may also touch the soul? Are not all these bits of culture derived from the same source? The cowboy hero does not preach the unity of culture: he demonstrates it. He is but one of many wellsprings of national experience. And as we translate his image from time to time on canvas, in film, in music, or on pages such as these, we move again toward definitions of ourselves. We will not likely achieve the clarity we desire, but the striving is what matters. The medium does not matter at all.

Addendum

Since the manuscript for this volume was delivered to the publisher, further indications of popular attention to cowboy

---

[29] George Bluestone, "The Changing Cowboy: From Dime Novel to Dollar Film," *Western Humanities Review* 14 (Summer, 1960): 337.

imagery have appeared. *Newsweek* featured Willie Nelson on its August 14, 1978, cover and published a five-page appreciation by Pete Axthelm. *Time* followed with a three-page piece in its issue of September 18, 1978. *Esquire* explored the contemporary image with Aaron Latham's "The Ballad of the Urban Cowboy: America's Search for True Grit" in its September 12, 1978, issue. NBC Television portrayed both sides of the coin in December, 1978, with Harvey Laidman's film *Steel Cowboy,* a cowboy-trucker mini-epic improved by superior performances by James Brolin and Rip Torn, and Burt Brinckerhoff's production of *Stubby Pringle's Christmas* for "Hallmark Hall of Fame," starring Beau Bridges as a cowboy who shows signs of growing up. And John Wayne courted controversy with his brand of cowboy wisdom once again when he advocated releasing Patty Hearst from prison. In comments to Barbara Walters shortly after the People's Temple deaths at Jonestown, Guyana, the Duke observed that "the American people have immediately accepted that one man can brainwash 400 human beings into mass suicide, but will not accept the fact that a ruthless group, the Symbionese Liberation Army, could brainwash one little girl." Shortly afterward John Wayne entered the hospital for stomach surgery. Cowboy actor Chill Wills died in Encino, California, on December 16, 1978; and Wayne died of cancer on June 11, 1979.

Appendix
A Cowboy
Chronology

This chronology is intended to demonstrate certain juxta-positions that may be useful to the reader contemplating the development of, and changes in, cowboy imagery in American culture. It does not pretend to completeness.

1857   Birth of William Levi ("Buck") Taylor in Fredericks-burg, Texas

1866   Long drives begin; first trail herds reach Abilene, Kansas, in 1867

1878   Publication of Arthur Morecamp's *The Live Boys; or, Charlie and Nasho in Texas,* the first instance of the use of the long drive as a theme in fiction

1883   Cowboys strike for higher wages in Texas Panhandle
        "Buffalo Bill's Wild West" opens its first season

1884   The Chisholm Trail ceases to be an important cattle artery
        William F. Cody introduces Buck Taylor, "King of Cowboys," to wild West audiences
        Theodore Roosevelt begins ranching in North Dakota

1887   Publication of Prentiss Ingraham's *Buck Taylor, King of the Cowboys* in Beadle's Half-Dime Library, the first appearance of the cowboy hero in fiction
Bill Pickett, at age sixteen, first demonstrates his bulldogging techniques

1888   Theodore Roosevelt publishes *Ranch Life and Hunting Trail,* lionizing cowboys

1890   Long drives end

1898   Cowboys enlist in First U.S. Volunteer Cavalry (the "Rough Riders") under Colonel Leonard Wood and Lieutenant Colonel Theodore Roosevelt for service in the war with Spain

1899   Theodore Roosevelt publishes *The Rough Riders,* lionizing cowboys

1902   Publication of Owen Wister's *The Virginian*

1903   Publication of Andy Adams's *The Log of a Cowboy*

1904   Will Rogers enters vaudeville

1907   Publication of Clarence Mulford's *Bar-20,* introducing Hopalong Cassidy

1914   Cecil B. DeMille directs the first film version of *The Virginian*

1915   William S. Hart's first movie appearance

1916   Last season of "Buffalo Bill's Wild West"

1917   Tom Mix's first feature movie appearance

1923   Publication of Emerson Hough's *North of 36*
Otto Gray, the first singing cowboy, begins performing with his band, the Oklahoma Cowboys

1924   Buck Taylor dies in Downingtown, Pennsylvania

1927   John Wayne's first movie appearance

A COWBOY CHRONOLOGY

1928   Randolph Scott's first movie appearance

1929   Victor Fleming directs the second film version of *The Virginian*

1930   John Wayne's first western, *The Big Trail*, directed by Raoul Walsh

1932   Death of Bill Pickett

1933   "The Tom Mix Ralston Straightshooters" premieres on radio

1934   Gene Autry's first movie appearance

1935   William Boyd appears in *Hop-A-Long Cassidy* (sic), the first of sixty-six Cassidy films

Death of Will Rogers

Roy Rogers's first movie appearance

1936   Tex Ritter's first movie appearance

The Cowboy's Turtle Association organized; the name changed to Rodeo Cowboys' Association in 1945

1940 "Gene Autry's Melody Ranch" premieres on radio
Death of Tom Mix

1944   "The Roy Rogers Show" premieres on radio

1946   Stuart Gilmore directs third film version of *The Virginian*

1948   The first appearance of William Boyd's Hopalong Cassidy films on television

1950   "Hopalong Cassidy" premieres on radio, January 1, starring William Boyd; three days later Hoppy begins as syndicated daily comic strip

"The Tom Mix Ralston Straightshooters" ends on radio

1951   William Boyd begins production of fifty-two half-hour television films to supplement his B-film programs

"The Gene Autry Show" begins a three-year television run on CBS

"The Roy Rogers Show" begins a six-year television run on NBC

1954   Release of the last western B film, *Two Guns and a Badge*, starring Wayne Morris

1955   The National Cowboy Hall of Fame and Western Heritage Center chartered

1959   "Rawhide" begins a seven-year television run on CBS
"Bonanza" begins a fourteen-year television run on NBC

1962   "The Virginian" begins as a television series

1968   Tom Gries directs *Will Penny*

1970   William Fraker directs *Monte Walsh*
The last television appearance of the Marlboro cowboy

1972   Death of William Boyd
Dick Richards directs *The Culpepper Cattle Co.*
Mark Rydell directs *The Cowboys*

1974   The death of Tex Ritter, ballyhooed as "America's Most Beloved Cowboy"

1975   The release of Willie Nelson's album, *Red Headed Stranger*

1976   The release of Waylon Jennings's record "My Heroes Have Always Been Cowboys" and Ed Bruce's "Mamas, Don't Let Your Babies Grow Up to Be Cowboys"

1978   John Wayne, recovering from open-heart surgery, receives more than 100,000 pieces of mail from fans and well-wishers

1979   The death of John Wayne, from cancer.

Bibliographical
Note

In ADDITION TO the sources cited in the footnotes, there are general reference works useful to the student of cowboy imagery. Guides to the bibliography of the historical cowboy are Ramon F. Adams, *The Rampaging Herd: A Bibliography of Books and Pamphlets on Men and Events in the Cattle Industry* (Norman: University of Oklahoma Press, 1959); and, especially for periodical literature, Henry E. Fritz, ed., "The Cattlemen's Frontier in the Trans-Mississippi West: An Annotated Bibliography," published in two parts in *Arizona and the West*, 14 (Spring, 1972): 45-70; (Summer, 1972): 169-90. One should consider also the commentaries of J. Frank Dobie, whose *Guide to Life and Literature of the Southwest,* (rev. ed.) (Dallas: Southern Methodist University Press, 1952), contains assessments of a great deal of published cowboy material, including memoirs and autobiographies, pamphlet literature, fiction, photographic collections, art books, biographies, and monographs. Chapter 21, entitled "Range Life," is the longest one in the book.

Richard W. Etulain, *Western American Literature: A Bibliography of Interpretive Books and Articles* (Vermillion, S.Dak.: Dakota Press, 1972), contains an extensive section on bibliographies and general works, as well as checklists of critical studies about western writers and writers of westerns. Representative cowboys (Andy Adams, Charles A. Siringo), image makers (Theodore Roosevelt, Owen Wister, Frederic Remington, Will Rogers), and popular writers (Clarence Mulford, Max Brand, Zane Grey) are among those included.

An indispensable guide to motion pictures is Leslie Halliwell, *The Filmgoer's Companion* (New York: Hill and Wang, 1966), which has improved in each of its several subsequent editions. Ronald Gottesman and Harry M. Geduld, *Guidebook to Film: An Eleven-in-One Reference* (New York: Holt, Rinehart and Winston, 1972), contains annotated topical bibliographies, lists of dissertations and theses pertaining to film, a directory of museums and archives, and directories of film distributors, film studios, book publishers, poster dealers, and so forth. Other useful references include Richard Roud, ed., *A Critical Dictionary of the Cinema,* 4 vols. (New York: Viking Press, 1978); and Liz-Ann Bawden, ed., *The Oxford Companion to Film* (New York: Oxford University Press, 1976).

Frank Buxton and Bill Owen, *The Big Broadcast, 1920-1950* (New York: Viking Press, 1972), deals with radio and supplements the previously cited work of John Dunning. Both claim to be complete, but neither is. For television see Vincent Terrace, *The Complete Encyclopedia of Television Programs,* 2 vols. (Cranbury, N.J.: A. S. Barnes, 1976): and Les Brown, *The New York Times Encyclopedia of Television* (New York: Times Books, 1977).

Maurice Horn, ed., *The World Encyclopedia of Comics* (New York: Chelsea House Publishers, 1976), explains in greater detail many of the particulars mentioned in Horn's previously cited study of western comics. An essential reference is Robert M. Overstreet, *The Comic Book Price Guide, 1977-1978,* 7th ed. (Cleveland, Tenn.: Published by the Author, 1977), because it is the best available index. Overstreet lists titles alphabetically and provides publishers and dates of publication with each entry. The guide is revised each year, but any edition will assist the student of cowboy imagery. It is distributed to the book trade by Harmony Books, a division of Crown Publishers, New York.

Irwin Stambler and Grelun Landon, *Encyclopedia of Folk, Country and Western Music* (New York: St. Martin's Press, 1969); and Melvin Shestack, *The Country Music Encyclopedia* (New York: Thomas Y. Crowell, 1974), are biographical references with brief discographies. Those in search of rare or obscure material can consult Jerry Osborne, *55 Years of Recorded Country/Western Music* (Phoenix, Ariz.: O'Sullivan Woodside & Company, 1976), which unfortunately does not contain release dates. Happily, however, it contains an interview with Gene Autry on the subject of his musical career.

Index

Abbey, Edward: 44
Abbott, E. C. ("Teddy Blue"): 5
Actors in cowboy roles: 28ff., 105
Adams, Andy: 5, 37, 138, 158
Adams, Jane: 100
Adams, Ramon: 39
Advertising, cowboy in: 115ff.,
    121-22
Alabama: 132
Albert, Allan: 163
Alger, Horatio, Jr.: 23, 152
"Along the Navajo Trail" (song):
    86
Amazing Rhythm Aces: 89
American Broadcasting
    Company: 131
American Humane
    Association: 41
"Annie Oakley" (television
    series): 106
Arizona: 42, 45, 46
Arkansas: 87
Arthur, Jean: 100
Askew, Luke: 34
Atherton, Lewis: 13
Austin, Texas: 82
Australia: 45

"Automotive western": 43ff
Autry, Gene: 47, 81, 85-88,
    100-101, 106, 147, 151&n.,
    152

Baltimore Colts: 132
Bama, James: 83n.
Bare, Bobby: 79
Barry, Don ("Red"): 29&n., 105
Bass, "Outlaw" Ron: 133-34
Beadle's Half-Dime Library: 111
Beard, Menford: 30-31
"Big Iron" (song): 88
"Big Valley, The" (television
    series): 105, 156
Billy the Kid (ballet suite): 163
Blacks as cowboys: 6ff.
Blake, Robert: 42-43
Blazing Saddles (film): 81n.
"Blue Prairie" (song): 86
"Blue Shadows on the Trail"
    (song): 86
Bluestone, George: 163
Boetticher, Budd: 130
"Bonanza" (television series):
    105, 131, 148, 156

173